SECRETS
TO
RECEIVING
UNCOMMON
BREAKTHROUGHS

SECRETS
TO
RECEIVING
UNCOMMON
BREAKTHROUGHS
Uncommon Breakthrough Prayer Points

SHEGUN BINO ALABI

ARPress
ILLUMINATING IDEAS
EMPOWERING VOICES

ARPress
45 Dan Road Suite 5
Canton MA 02021
Hotline: 1(888) 821-0229
Fax: 1(508) 545-7580

Ordering Information:
Quantity sales. Special discounts are available on quantity purchases by corporations, associations, and others. For details, contact the publisher at the address above.

Printed in the United States of America.

ISBN-13: Paperback   979-8-89389-036-5
          eBook   979-8-89389-037-2

Library of Congress Control Number: 2024912239

CONTENTS

About the Author vii

Preface..ix

Introduction...xi

Chapter 1   Who to pray for daily!.........................1

Chapter 2   Why do we pray?.................................4

Chapter 3   Mysteries and Secrets.........................7

Chapter 4   The Lord's Prayer...............................8

Chapter 5   Effective Prayer................................12

Chapter 6   Guarantee Answers to Prayers!.........17

Chapter 7   Divine Favor....................................18

Chapter 8   Strongest Foes.................................21

Chapter 9   Protection..24

Chapter 10   Barrenness......................................27

Chapter 11   Promotion.......................................30

Chapter 12   Household Enemies........................33

Chapter 13   Stagnation......................................36

Chapter 14   Burdened Heart...............................39

Chapter 15   Open Heaven..................................42

Chapter 16   Fear..45

Chapter 17   Shame and Reproach......................48

Chapter 18   Deliverance....................................51

Chapter 19   Binding and Casting Away..............54

Chapter 20   Anointing.......................................57

Chapter 21   Winds of God.................................59

Chapter 22   Forgiveness....................................62

Chapter 23 Prayer for the Nation 65
Chapter 24 Power of God 68
Chapter 25 Foundational Powers..............71
Chapter 26 Inherited Powers..............74
Chapter 27 Imaginations and Thoughts 77
Chapter 28 Limitation Forces 80
Chapter 29 Evil Altars..............83
Chapter 30 Divine Altars 86
Chapter 31 Powers Against Churches..............89
Chapter 32 Restoration..............92
Chapter 33 Safe Travels 95
Chapter 34 Completion..............98
Chapter 35 Uncommon and Unusual Success..............101
Chapter 36 Opened Eyes and Ears..............104
Chapter 37 Thanksgiving Prayer Points..............107
Chapter 38 Celestial Powers..............110
Chapter 39 Decrees and Declarations 113
Chapter 40 Prayers for Leader 116
Chapter 41 Prayers for Nations, States, and Cities..............120
Chapter 42 Destiny Destroyers 123
Chapter 43 Breaking Chains 126
Chapter 44 Trees of Life..............129
Chapter 45 Covenant 132
Chapter 46 Repentance Prayer after Disobedience..............135
Chapter 47 Tongues of God..............138
Chapter 48 Kill or Give Life 141
Chapter 49 Speaking in unknown tongues 145
Chapter 50 Praise..............147
Chapter 51 What Christians Must Know!..............151
Chapter 52 Conclusion..............153
Chapter 53 Heaven's Court..............155

ABOUT THE AUTHOR

The Author, Shegun Bino Alabi was born in Nigeria and he moved to the USA in early 1990. He is an Evangelist and he was raised in a Christian home. His father was also an Evangelist. He backslidden as soon as he moved out of his parents' house. He was subsequently rearrested by Jesus in 1990. He lived as a lukewarm Christian for many years, playing church (Go to church every Sunday, and Wednesday, and paying tithes) and also living a worldly life. He finally decided to live for Christ when he met his wife, Helen Alabi, in 2008.

Author received a diploma after completing four-year training in a School of Ministry organized by the International Pentecostal Holiness Churches of America in 2005 and he has attended several seminary classes as a minister.

One night the author was awoken by an Angel who took him into a place that looked like heaven, climbed stairs out of the roof of their house into this open world and into heaven-like setting and he was introduced to Jesus Christ. The Angel said, "Can you see that Jesus is alive"? And Mr. Alabi said yes, I can see that Jesus is alive, and the Angel said, "Now go and tell the whole world that Jesus is alive." Jesus did not interrupt the conversation, but was simply looking on. It may have been Jesus who asked the Angel to go bring the author to be baptized into evangelism ministry. That was the beginning of the author's evangelism ministry.

He is currently an Evangelist and assisting the Pastors (Pastor Chris Ethekpemhi and Pastor Mrs. Evelyn Ethakpemhi) at God's Glorious Praise Ministry at 17808 Sierra Highway, Canyon Country, CA 91351. This is the 3rd ministry that God is using the author to assist in planting. His Ministry is Evangelism and church planting. He has a wife, six children and a grandchild – Bridget, Naomi, Nora, Amara, Daniel and Daniella and his grand-daughter, Timmy Useh.

PREFACE

The author, Shegun Bino Alabi, in writing this book, received inspiration and help from these sources: God gave me the inspiration for this book and the writings are moves from God to give Power, Faith, and Knowledge to every user of it. God directed me to write this book, therefore, all glory goes to Him. This book will benefit those who USE it. All glory, honor, and praise go to God for helping us complete the writing and publication.

Special thanks to my wife, Helen Alabi, who supported me with prayers and always spurring me to get up and complete the book. My daughter, Naomi Alabi, was urging me to spend the money it takes to publish the book for the benefit of the world. My little ones Daniel Alabi and Daniella Alabi, were helping me to find and read the Bible versions.

God gave me a vision in the middle of the night and told me I should write this book, so that anyone who uses it will get Uncommon Breakthroughs in all endeavors of their lives. The Holy Spirit told me that this book is a Blessing! This handbook is not intended to replace reading the Bible, but it is a book you should have in your car and home along with your Bible. Use them both, because your life may well depends on them.

Daniel Alabi and Daniella Alabi were my helpers in reading the different Bible versions that I used - they were quick to let me hear those versions again and again before I decided the version I preferred to use. All quotes are either from the King James

Bible version, New King James version, Amplified Version, The New Living Translation, and The Message Version. I can't thank these children enough for their immense help. God bless you and I pray that God will continue to support you the way you have supported your father in this work.

INTRODUCTION

Background as to how prayers are answered

I have met a lot of Christians who say they do not know how to pray and their prayers are so limited to a few prayer points. I have also met Christians who say they can pray 12 hours straight, only if they have the time. I have met Christians who pray at least two hours every day. Do you have to learn how to pray or someone needs to teach you how to pray? I thought I should also, with this introduction, lay out areas you can pray about.

What is Prayer?

Prayer is a communication with God, our maker. Prayer is having a fellowship with our heavenly father, our Lord and the owner of our souls. Prayer is intercession for others, friends, relatives, nations, cities, and whenever you mention another entity to God in prayer is intercession. Most importantly, prayer is interaction with the Almighty God. Most people tend to end their prayer quickly, because they don't have a great relationship with God, so they come to His presence and leave after asking for a solution to one thing they know is bothering them or what they consider to be their only need. We should use prayer time to create a relationship with God. He gets to know you and you get to know Him more.

Our Relationship equal our prayer. Our style of prayer brings to my mind the relationship my wife and I have with our Chinese exchange students. They could not speak English and we could not speak Chinese, so when they come to see us, they have rehearsed what to say to us and how to say it. They have already typed the question on Chinese translation software. So, if they did not know how to ask, they would simply show us in writing what they need. This is how most of us are with God. We do not have daily fellowship with God, so when we come before God, we ask for solutions to the one thing or more problems troubling us and we quickly run off. Sometimes we show little thanks in form of gratitude to get Him off our backs and to prove to ourselves that we have satisfied the routine.

These moments are not quality times and are not true fellowship. God needs our time for fellowship and interactions.

What does God want?

God is looking for men and women who will spend time with Him and not look at their clocks and watches. Hearing from God can only come when you sacrifice quality time with Him in fellowship. When we pray, we should always expect to hear back from God and hearing from God can only come when you ask Him to speak to you after prayer and fellowship times. I implore you to dedicate time away from TV and spend the time with your maker.

Why is faith necessary?

We need to ask, why the Bible did, say "... The effective fervent prayer of a righteous man avails much" - James 5:16?

There are different kinds of prayers; some are fervent and effective and those are the ones that produce results. Others are not fervent and ineffective and therefore they produce no result. What type of prayers do you pray?

Why some people enjoy uncommon breakthroughs?

This Uncommon Breakthrough Prayer Points Handbook is meant to be a guide as to the areas that you may need to cover in prayers, but are often times missed or neglected. Sometimes, we may never even think to cover these areas when we have no guide such as this book or we do not even know that these areas exist.

Nevertheless, the Spirit intercedes for us through speaking in tongues, but knowing some of these prayer points would greatly improve the effectiveness of your prayers and prayer life. It is important for us to know how to pray.

Prayer is very important.

The Disciples of Jesus requested that he teaches them how to pray according to - Luke 11:1. They could have asked Jesus Christ to teach them how to perform miracles, but they asked Jesus to teach them how to pray. That is to prove to us how important knowing how to pray is. The Bible did not say if we pray, but it says when we pray.

"Man always ought to pray and not faint...." - Luke 18:1: Jesus Christ also emphasized on the need for a Christian to have a consistent prayer life.

CHAPTER 1

WHO TO PRAY FOR DAILY!

When you pray, you should not forget these areas:

(I will expound on it in the subject titled how to pray an effective prayer).

1. Pray for yourself.
2. Pray for your family – Your wife and children – Thank God for their lives and pray that they have a great day today.
   a. Thank God for waking you up and that you are able to see the day.
   b. Worshipping God's greatness.
   c. Ask God to forgive you of your sins.
   d. Ask God to help you to forgive others – this should come before asking God to forgive you of your own sins.
   e. Committing your day into the hands of God is a big deal. God wants to be in all of our affairs, because He wants us to acknowledge Him in all of our ways.
   f. Committing your objectives of the day should be a priority - what you planned to do today should be committed to God.
   g. God asks us to command the day to favor us, so that the evil of that day would be shaken away from our day - Job 38:12-13.

3. If you have no wife and children, but hope to have a family one day, commit them to God. Thank God for giving you a good wife who would know God, fear God, love God, and love you.

4. Pray for your friends – Job in the Bible received his own breakthrough after he prayed for his friends.

5. Pray for your neighbors – Even if you think they are your enemies. Ask God to bless your neighbors and ask God to supply the needs of your neighbors.

6. If a neighbor has a specific prayer need that you are aware of, pray for them; even if they did not ask you to pray for them.

7. Pray for your church members – Generally and specifically, if you know of a specific need, let that need of the member become your own burden according to the Bible. "Bear burdens of each other." - Galatians 6:2.

8. Pray for the leaders of your church – Aaron and Hur helped Moses to keep his hands up – Exodus 17:12.

9. Pray for the President and the Governors – even if you do not agree with their policies and politics or that they belong to one party that is different from your own. All you are doing is obeying God, rather than yourself.

10. Pray for church workers; Pastors, Missionaries, evangelists all over the world. Pray that God continues to help and use them for his work.

11. Pray for the peace of this country and foreign countries, and the entire world.

12. Pray for poor people – those who are less privileged to have food, shelter, and more, today.

13. Pray that the rich will help the poor people.

14. Pray for justice for all – many people are going to jail daily because they have no good representations and that the under-privileged are not jailed unnecessarily.

15. Pray for those who are sick and shut in that they receive the healing touch of God.
16. Pray for the forgiveness of sins for your country and other countries.
17. Pray against the enemies of your country – That God will bring peace between the two countries.
18. Pray for your church – for a united church and a faithful church.
19. Pray that everyone at your church and other churches know God better than they do now according to - Jeremiah 9:24.
20. Pray that God sends down revival to all flesh – Revival is a time to audit activities of our lives.
21. Pray for opportunities for those committing crimes to come to repentance of their crimes and deliberate evil actions.
22. Pray for the unity of your church and other churches that we are all in one accord ("...That we speak the same thing and we are perfectly joined in the same mind and in the same judgment"). – 1 Corinthians 1: 10.
23. Pray that God sends down his Spirit of love upon all flesh.
24. Pray against killings of other humans by criminals and that God should help stop these activities. Pray against human trafficking and sex trafficking.
25. Pray that God does not allow the devil to have his way today.
26. Pray that God takes control of the hearts of our children, your own and others, as they are growing up.
27. Remember that giving and receiving is a product of a relationship. You give to those you have a relationship and they also give to you, because they have a relationship with you. Do not forget to have a relationship with God. That is the reason Jesus wants to be your friend – John 15:14.

CHAPTER 2

WHY DO WE PRAY?

"...Men always ought to pray and not faint" -Luke 18:1.

Prayer is expressing your belief or your faith in God to God.
Prayer is spending time with God and communicating with God.
We pray, because we recognize that there is power greater than our own.
We pray, because we know we have a maker who is alive and well.
We pray, because we recognize the power of our maker.

We pray, because we cannot do a specific thing for ourselves.
We pray, because we know of Divine powers.
We pray, because we know the existence of angels.
We pray, because we know that there is power in the unseen world.

We pray, because we admit our shortcomings.
We pray, because there must be something that exist that you don't know about.
We pray, because we are wise.
We pray, because we need a touch that you have not received yet.

We pray, because we need to feel the love that we do not feel now.
We pray, because we need an embrace from higher powers, which we are not currently feeling.

We pray, because we believe in God.
We pray, because we have faith.
We pray, because we have tried others.

We pray, because we love God.
We pray, because we believe God loves us.
We pray, because we are weak.
We pray, because we accept our weakness.
We pray, because we need help.

We pray, because there is vagueness in our lives.
We pray, because you need clarity.
We pray, because you need what is happening around you to stop.
We pray, because you need to overcome.

We pray, because we believe we can do better than this.

We pray, because we don't know why we remain where we are.
We pray, because we need to move forward.
We pray, because we have exhausted our efforts.

We pray, because we have asked our fathers with no satisfactory answer.
We pray, because we have asked our mothers and she gave us no satisfactory answer.
We pray, because we have asked all of our relatives and they gave us no satisfactory answer.
We pray, because we have asked our friends and they gave us no satisfactory answer.
We pray, because we have exhausted our personal resources.

We pray, because we need to maintain a stronger relationship with our maker – God.

5

We pray, because even Jesus Christ started with prayer and ended with prayer.

We pray, because God says if we pray he will answer us.

We pray, because if there is a man to pray, there is a God to answer.

CHAPTER 3

MYSTERIES AND SECRETS

"And He said, to you it is given to know the Mysteries of the Kingdom of God: but to them that are outside, all these things are done in parables" - Mark 4:11.

The Kingdom of God is a mystery that can only be entered into by revelation. It is only through revelation that you can have understanding and through understanding you can access the power behind the mysteries of the Kingdom of God and the power behind it.

The Bible is a mystery book that it takes unstoppable search for the revelation, before it would begin to be revealed to you.

i.   "Let a man so consider us, as servants of Christ and stewards of the mysteries of God - 1 Corinthians 4:1.
ii. "The mystery which has been hidden from ages and from generations, but now has been revealed to His saints -Colossians 1:26.
iii. "...The mystery of God would be finished, as He declared to His servants and prophets Revelation 10:7.
iv. Again, the Kingdom of God is a mystery and to receive from it, you need revelation and this book is here to provide some of the revelations.

CHAPTER 4

THE LORD'S PRAYER

This is only a model prayer – Areas we should touch when we are praying.

This is how Jesus taught his disciples to pray:
Matthew 6: 9 - 13

"In this manner, therefore, pray:

Our Father in heaven, Hallowed be Your name
Your kingdom come Your will be done
On earth as it is in Heaven
Give us this day our daily bread
And forgive us our debts, as we forgive our debtors
And do not lead us into temptation, but deliver us from the evil one.
For yours is the kingdom and the power and the glory forever, Amen".

Jesus Christ came to introduce God to us as our father.
Here are the areas we should cover when we are praying for you and praying for others.
Here, Jesus lets us know that we should acknowledge God as our Divine Father who is in Heaven and who has power on earth.

We should worship His greatness, by letting Him know He is Holy and the only One.

Pray for His kingdom to come into your life and His will be done, because the will of God is good for all of us. God's will is what rules in heaven and we want the same will to rule here on earth and in our lives.

We should look only to God for our daily cares, food, and all of our other life needs. God knows our needs, but we need to let Him know that we depend on him for all of our needs.

Asking God for help keeps us humble and submissive to His will. Most importantly to God (Our Holy Father) is that we live Holy, but since we really cannot, we need to ask God to forgive us of all of our sins, but we should also forgive those who have wronged us.

Without forgiveness of other people including our friends and family members who have wronged us, we cannot be forgiven by God. Forgiveness of sins is very important to God and that is the reason God sent His only begotten son, Jesus Christ, to die to reconcile us to Himself. It is not easy to forgive, but we forgive, because it is a commandment of God and also because we want to be forgiven, so that we can be cleaned before God.

Forgiving others is not our will, but the will of God and when we do, we are obeying God. There is 'true forgiveness' and there is 'lip forgiveness'. 'Lip forgiveness' is forgiveness that is shallow and every time you remember what happened, you are again in pain from what happened to you. 'True forgiveness' only comes when you begin to pray for those who hurt you. Pray for those who hurt you until you overcome the wrong done to you. Practice and practice and practice and you would be perfect at it.

We want God to lead us away from temptation, because our flesh will not turn away from lustful desires. It is only the Spirit of God in us that can help lead us away from committing sin.

Deliver us from evil – We contend with evil on a daily bases, the Bible describes it this way: "For we wrestle not against flesh and blood, but against principalities, against powers, against the rulers of darkness in the heavenly places" - Ephesians 6: 12.

The devil is our enemy. All other forces that fight with us are nothing but messengers of Satan, such as demons, witches, wizards, and all kinds of unseen powers to demote, dethrone, alter, frustrate, stagnate, destroy, kills, inflict diseases, destroy the destinies of humans and to make sure we do not fulfill our purpose and destiny and that is why we need powers that can fight for us. It is not a war or battle against another human being, but against unseen powers. So, every time you fight with anyone, it is "the enemy" pushing the person against you. Do not fight, but go and commit the situation to God. When you do that you are addressing the spiritual side of what's going on.

Finally, acknowledge the fact that God is the creator, our maker, the owner of everything in the earth and heaven. God is the beginning and the end, the everlasting power that cannot and would never die. He is a King that cannot be dethroned. God would live forever and ever, period!

He is always on the throne, whether we live or die. God is forever the everlasting King and His throne is from generation to generation – better find your place in Him.

You should never be angry with God, because your anger would neither dethrone Him nor alter who He is. Knowing God is for us; in order to make our short lives here on earth pleasant.

CHAPTER 5

EFFECTIVE PRAYER

"The effective fervent prayer of a righteous man avails much" - James 5:16.

This topic is a message in itself, but I have shortened it to fit this space, because this is a prayer book with mostly prayer points.

To call on God at all as a Christian, you must be born again: Jesus answered and said to him, "Most assuredly, I say to you, unless one is born again, he cannot see the kingdom of God" – John 3:3.

Do not close the door of God's love for you, so, declare as below:

Accept Jesus as Lord and Savior

a. I declare that Jesus Christ died for me and by His death He washed away my sins.
b. Jesus Christ's death, burial, and resurrection were all done for me.
c. From today, I accept Jesus Christ into my life as my Lord and Savior and when I die I will be with Him in Heaven. From today, my name is now written in the book of life. After sincerely receiving Jesus Christ as your Lord and Savior, when the father looks at you, He sees Jesus.

Your prayer is in the will of God:

"Therefore do not be unwise, but understand what the will of the Lord is" - Ephesians 5:17.

You should find out if your prayer is in line with God's will, before, during, and after you pray.

i. Is your issue addressed in the Bible?(Express will)
ii. What would Jesus say about your situation? Would Jesus intervene and help you or He would allow you to suffer?

    a. There is a place in the Bible where God addressed your issue.
    b. Your prayer is not outside what God desires for you.
    c. Your prayer is tested and passed as what God would do for you.
    d. God says you should put him in remembrance of His word.

There is something in it for God (examples):

    a. If you are telling God that you are tired of riding taxis to church or tired of asking church members for rides to church; you are asking God for a car.
    b. If you want to pay more tithes – you are asking for a raise.
    c. If you are asking God that you want to start paying tithe – you are asking God for a job.
    d. If you are asking to raise a child after God – you are asking for a child.
    e. If are telling God that you want to support more ministries around the world – you are asking for financial increase.

Pray in humility

"Humble yourself under the mighty hands of God and he will exalt you in due times" – 1 Peter 5:6. "By humility and the fear of God are riches, honor, and life" – Proverbs 22:4:

a. So many times the Bible talks about the blessing God has for those who humble themselves.
b. Don't come before God in arrogance.
c. Humble yourself – "...If my people who are called by my name will humble themselves and pray and seek my face, I will hear, forgive their sins and restore their land..." -2 Chronicles 7: 14: or heal your situation or attend to your needs.
d. Know that you can't do it yourself, that is why you are praying to the higher power.

Produce your cause – Isaiah 41:21:

Visit a courthouse and see what a typical volume of a complaint looks like. God is also asking you why He should hear this request you are putting before him.

a. Show God why He should answer your prayer.
b. Support your prayer with Bible verses.
c. If God has done the same thing for Bible personnel, remind God – You did it for Sarah, Hannah, Jabez, Moses, etc.
d. Be sincere. No one can fool God.
e. Let your petition be from your heart, your spirit, from "the deep". "...Deep calls unto the deep...." - Psalm 42: 7.
f. Again, ask in humility: "The Lord takes pleasure in his people and He would beautify the humble with salvation" – Psalm 149:4.

g. Let your request not be to satisfy the flesh, to satisfy your pride, so you become the envy of others.

h. Do not let your request be 'seeking God to use God to satisfy your need' and then dump Him.

For example, you pray for a child or work and when your prayer is answered; you now use it as a reason why you do not come to church anymore.

Thanksgiving

"Be anxious for nothing, but in everything by prayer and supplication with thanksgiving, let your requests be made known to God." – Philippians 4: 6.

a. Thank God for what he has done for you in the past.

b. Thank God that He has already done it "Whatsoever you desire, when you pray, believe that you receive them and you shall have them." – Mark 11: 24: If you can't set your mind on having what you pray about, please don't ask. Jesus Christ said more will be added to those who have.

c. Thank God for what he is doing right now.

d. Let God know that it is His word, and that He does not fail to deliver when it is according to His word.

e. "Enter into His gate with thanksgiving Psalm 100:4. Come to God with an attitude of Thanksgiving.

Persist, persist, and persist – Read the story at Mark 7:

25 – 29: The woman refused to let Jesus go, despite Jesus denying to giving her the miracle she came to seek. She persisted until she received breakthrough for her daughter.

Another Story in the Bible is in Luke 18:1- 5: The unjust judge gave the widow whatever the widow was troubling the judge to receive from the judge. She received all that she needed.

a. After asking, begin thanking Him.

b. Thank Him until you have it in your hands.

c. Do not let age be an excuse – whether old or young.

d. Do not let your level of education be an excuse.

e. Let no association deter you from your goal to receive from God.

f. Let no external voice stop you.

g. Do not let yourself stand on your own way.

h. The color of your skin is never an excuse.

i. Just because you are born again, you qualify.

j. Forgive yourself and others and continue to ask.

k. The way you speak is not an excuse, Moses tried that excuse, and it did not work for him.

CHAPTER 6

GUARANTEE ANSWERS TO PRAYERS!

Always remember that the name of Jesus is the key to enter into the door of prayers.

Jesus said, "...Whatever you ask the Father in my name, He will give it to you" - John 16:23.

"Therefore I say to you, whatever things you ask when you pray, believe that you receive them, and you will have them" - Mark 11:24.

"Now God worked unusual miracles by the hands of Paul, so that even handkerchiefs or aprons were brought from his body to the sick, and the diseases left them and the evil spirits went out of them." – Acts 19:11:

1. Father Lord, thank you for answering my prayers as I pray, in Jesus name.
2. Heavenly father, give me the faith to know that my prayers are already answered as I pray now, in Jesus name.
3. Faith: Jesus said unto him, if thou canst believe, all things are possible to him that believeth.

CHAPTER 7

DIVINE FAVOR

"And I will give this people favor in the sight of the Egyptians; and it shall be, when you go, that you shall not go empty handed". - Exodus 3:21.

1. Lord, help me to realize that I need you, in Jesus name.
2. Lord, I can do nothing without you, so help me, in Jesus name.
3. For you created me to need help Lord, therefore, help me Lord, in Jesus name.
4. If you don't help me, for no one else can help me, so hear me Lord, in Jesus name.
5. I do not lean on a man, but you O' Lord, help me to lean on you, in Jesus name.
6. Create room of favor for me to lean on, in Jesus name.
7. The hearts of kings are in your hands, so sway them to favor me O' Lord, in Jesus name.
8. Let my help come from heaven alone, O' Lord, in Jesus name.
9. My Lord, help me to surrender completely to your will alone, O' Lord, in Jesus name.
10. Help me abide in you O' Lord, in Jesus name.
11. Come in Lord and abide in me, in Jesus name.
12. Help me hear your voice, so I can open my door to your favor O' Lord, in Jesus name.
13. Prepare me Lord to receive your favor, in Jesus name.

14. Prepare my foundation to hold your favors and blessings O' Lord, in Jesus name.
15. My God supply my needs out of your abundant grace, in Jesus name.
16. Lord, restore good health to me out of your grace, in Jesus name.
17. O' Lord favor me financially from unexpected source, in Jesus name.
18. O' Lord favor me when I meet with men, in Jesus name.
19. Father, help me find favor with women, in Jesus name.
20. Father, help me destroy powers in my foundation meant to hinder my favors, in Jesus name.
21. Father, remove obstacles that limit favors meant for me, in Jesus name.
22. Father, remove veil that drapes over the eyes of those that are supposed to favor me, in Jesus name.
23. Father, let those destined to favor me to locate me, in Jesus name.
24. Father, remove peace from my Divine helpers until they find me and favor me, in Jesus name.
25. Father, bless those who favor me, in Jesus name.
26. Father Lord, usher in your Divine favor into my life, in Jesus name.
27. Father, help me to live in your Divine favor, the rest of my life, in Jesus name.
28. Heavenly father, help me to use your favors to bring others to you, in Jesus name.
29. Father, help me never to forget to give the glory of your favor to you, in Jesus name.
30. Father, use me also to favor others, in Jesus name.
31. My Lord, open your heaven of favors unto others who love you Lord, in Jesus name.

Father Lord, open your heaven, so I can receive your favor wherever I go, in the mighty name of Jesus. . My Lord my God, bless me with your favor as I go out and when as I return, in Jesus name. . My Lord, I need your favor as I go to meet these people, in Jesus name. . My Lord, bless me with your favor, because I need your favor in order to come out of this situation, in Jesus name. . Father Lord, surround me with your favor as a shield, in

Jesus name. . Heavenly father, favor me and open every door the enemy closed against me, in Jesus name. . By your favor O' Lord rescue me from the trap I found myself, in Jesus name. . By your favor O' Lord open heavenly resources into my life, in Jesus name. . Powers frustrating my efforts; let them begin to favor me now, in Jesus name. . Let my adversaries become stepping stones into my successes, in Jesus name.

CHAPTER 8

STRONGEST FOES

People who are the closest to us are our strongest enemies, because they know all your secrets - These are close friends and family members:

"A man's enemies will be the members of his own household" - Matthew 10:36.

"When the wicked, even mine enemies and my foes came upon me to eat up my flesh, they stumbled and fell". - Psalm 27:2:

1. From today every power from within my household controlling my life is moved out, in Jesus name.
2. Every remote influence and control by family wicked member is stopped today, in Jesus name.
3. I release my life from chains caused by family members, in Jesus name.
4. Every intentional or unintentional act of family members that could cause my downfall, I break out of it today, in Jesus name.
5. Every act of my father that will affect my life, I paralyze it today, in the name of Jesus.
6. Every act by my mother that will affect my life negatively, I detach myself from it today, in Jesus name.
7. Every Intentional and unintentional acts of my father to change my destiny is reversed today, in Jesus name.

8. Every failures of my father shall not affect me, in Jesus name.

9. I distance myself from my parents' failures, in Jesus name.

10. All failures of my mother shall not affect me, in Jesus name.

11. I bring a gap between me and my mother's failures, in Jesus name.

12. I bring a gap between me and my father's failures in, Jesus name.

13. The powers set up against my father that stopped him from achieving his heights shall have nothing to do with me, in Jesus name.

14. The Powers that limited my mother shall not affect me, in Jesus name.

15. Every Association of my father that brought him disgrace shall not affect me, in Jesus name.

16. Every association by my mother that stopped her at her break through points is not my portion, in Jesus name.

17. Sicknesses of my mother are not my own, in Jesus name.

18. Sicknesses of my father are not my own, in Jesus name.

19. Every family evil associations of my father's house are deleted from my own life, in Jesus name.

20. Every evil associations of my mother's house are deleted from my family, in Jesus name.

21. Every Goliath shall become my steps to rise up, in Jesus name.

22. Powers I opened the doors to, intentionally or unintentionally are rebuked and cast out, in Jesus name.

23. Enemies who pretend to be friends are exposed and disgraced, in Jesus name.

24. Powers assigned to me from birth, their times have expired, in Jesus name.

25. Powers that have always stopped members of my household are destroyed, in Jesus name.

26. Powers that can invoke my spirit, you are destroyed, in Jesus name.

27. Powers that can chant with celestial powers to destroy others, I am untouchable, in Jesus name.

28. Garments that were sown for me to redirect my life affairs are burnt by the fire of God, in Jesus name.

29. Demonic powers that have written rights into my life, you are stopped, in Jesus name.

30. Foundational powers that ruled and reigned in my father's house for over two thousand years, I command that your powers are stopped now, in Jesus name.

31. Eternal powers that were given rights of passage into my mother, before I was born, your time is up, in Jesus name.

32. Powers that represented god in my mother's house or my father's house are paralyzed now, in Jesus name.

33. You unstoppable powers that ruled the geography of wherever I live, you are chased out, in Jesus name.

34. Powers that use the word of God to limit or stop me, you are hereby stopped, in Jesus name.

35. Let the anointing of God protect and shield me and my household, in Jesus name.

CHAPTER 9

PROTECTION

"...Unless the Lord guards the city, the watchman stays awake in vain." Psalm 127:1b.

1. Lord, help me to depend on you for protection, in Jesus name.
2. My father, help me to believe that you can and you would protect me, in Jesus name.
3. Father, help me to know that even with a gun, only you can protect me from harm, in Jesus name.
4. Father, help me to depend on your eyes watching over me day and night, in Jesus name.
5. O' Lord protect me from evil as I leave home this morning, in Jesus name.
6. Father, order my footsteps today, so as to avoid any road thirsty for blood, in Jesus name.
7. As a household, we depend on you for our security, therefore do not let any member of my family expose us to evil, in Jesus name.
8. My Lord, protect my family even as I leave behind at home, in Jesus name.
9. Lord, honor your word to me that you would set your men around our walls day and night, in Jesus name.
10. My father, when enemies come at me, please raise up your standard against them, in Jesus name.
11. Oh Lord, always be on my side, so as to remain secured in your arms, in Jesus name.

12. O' Lord, protect my interest even when am not there, in Jesus name.

13. Father, you promised that my judgments are canceled, therefore protect me from the effects of the judgments of man, in Jesus name.

14. Those who put their trust in the Lord are safe, help me to put all my trust in you O' Lord my God, in Jesus name.

15. Father, increase my faith in you that you would protect me, in Jesus name.

16. Father, protect my physical and spiritual being, in Jesus name.

17. Father, protect my blessings; even make them invincible to satanic knowledge in Jesus name.

18. Father, protect my star from evil attacks, in Jesus name.

19. Father, protect my born and unborn children, in Jesus name.

20. My Lord, I surrender my destiny in your hands, therefore protect it for me O' Lord, in Jesus name.

21. My Lord, protect my source of income from my enemies, in Jesus name.

22. My Lord, protect me when am at work and take me home safely, in Jesus name.

23. Heavenly father, protect my visions, my dreams, and my aspirations, in Jesus name.

24. My father, protect me from natural disasters, in Jesus name.

25. My Lord, protect me from human mistakes, in Jesus name.

26. My Lord, protect me from every pit laid ahead for me or for others, in Jesus name.

27. Father, protect me from every evil that may await me, in Jesus name.

28. Father, protect my Salvation and faith, in Jesus name.

29. Father, save me from those who hate me, in Jesus name.
30. Father, help me remain more than a conqueror, in Jesus name.
31. No weapon formed against me shall prosper, in Jesus name.
32. Father Lord, let the Goliath of my life not consume me, in Jesus name.
33. Father Lord, protect my church building from harm by haters of Christian houses, in Jesus name.
34. Heavenly Father, protect my family even when am away from home, in Jesus name.
35. Father Lord, please protect the destiny of my siblings from being exchanged, in Jesus name.
36. Father Lord, protect my steps not to enter into the wrong house, in Jesus name.
37. Heavenly father, let your protection cover me even when I eat from the wrong hands, in Jesus name.
38. Almighty God, do not take your protection from us even when my children make the wrong choice, in Jesus name.
39. O' Lord, protect our names in the book of life, in Jesus name.
40. Father Lord, please protect your interest in me now and always, in Jesus name.

CHAPTER 10

BARRENNESS

"No one shall suffer miscarriage or barren in your land and I will fulfill the number of your days". Exodus 23: 26.

"You shall be blessed above all people; there shall not be male or female barren amongst you or your livestock." Deuteronomy 7:14.

1. It is your will that no one is barren amongst us; therefore remove barrenness from us, in Jesus name.
2. Father, let not my land or my career suffer barrenness, in Jesus name.
3. I commit my marriage in your hands that we shall be fruitful and not be barren, in Jesus mighty name.
4. I commit the womb of my wife in your hands that her womb shall produce the fruit of the womb, in Jesus powerful name.
5. Father, let no wicked men dwell amongst me to turn my land or career into barrenness, in Jesus name.
6. Father, transfer my barrenness to my enemies, in Jesus name.
7. Father, help me to be fruitful, so I will not be cut down, in Jesus name.
8. Father, help me cut down every tree that is not bearing fruits in my life, in Jesus name.
9. Father, help me avoid money-pit investments, in Jesus name.

10. Heavenly Father, I want to be your fruitful servant, therefore lead me to the career, business that you have appointed for me, in Jesus name.

11. Father, reveal to me where to be in order to avoid barrenness, in Jesus name.

12. You promised that everyone bears two and no one shall be barren, so grant to me double blessings in all that I do including child bearing, in Jesus name (Songs of Solomon 4:2).

13. Father, increase my faith, so I would overcome barrenness, in Jesus name.

14. Father, release my hidden treasures and talents, so I can achieve my maximum fruitfulness, in Jesus name.

15. Father, keep me away from the land of barrenness, in Jesus name.

16. Father, lead me to the land of fruitfulness, in Jesus name.

17. Heavenly father, protect me from associations that would cause me to be barren, in Jesus name.

18. Father, remove from me ancestral ties that would cause me to be barren, in Jesus name.

19. Heavenly father, detach me from any curse that would make me to be barren, in Jesus name.

20. Father, do not let me associate with barrenness of my father's house or my mother's house, in Jesus name.

21. Father Lord, break down walls that want to keep me barren, in Jesus name.

22. Your word says that you will make the dry land springs of water, father water my land, in Jesus name. (Isaiah 41:18).

23. Lord, open your window of heaven and pour me a blessing I shall not have room to receive, in Jesus name.

24. Father Lord, fix my foundation, so that I can avoid barrenness, in Jesus name.

25. Heavenly father, prepare my foundation for your blessing, in Jesus name.
26. Almighty father, destroy powers set up to keep me barren, in Jesus name.
27. Father Lord, help me avoid going to places that would create barrenness in my life, in Jesus name.
28. Heavenly father, help me locate where I would not be barren, in Jesus name.
29. Father Lord, help me receive instructions from you that would make me fruitful, in Jesus name.
30. Heavenly father, Help me maintain your anointing to keep me fruitful all the days of my life, in Jesus name.
31. Father Lord, uncover your mercy on all my children, so that barrenness is not their testimony, in Jesus name.
32. Let barrenness be far from our congregation, in Jesus name.
33. I break the spirit of barrenness holding onto your children, in Jesus name.
34. I send the spirit of barrenness back to where it came from, in Jesus name.
35. Father Lord, let barrenness no longer be the testimony of your children, in Jesus name.

CHAPTER 11

PROMOTION

"For promotion comes neither from the east nor from the west, nor from the south." –Psalm 75: 6.

"You have circled this mountain long enough, now turn northward". –Deuteronomy 2:3:

1. Father, promote me O' Lord, because promotion comes from you alone, in Jesus name.
2. Heavenly father, move me forward, because I have had enough of this place, in Jesus name.
3. It is your will for us to prosper, therefore prosper me more than where I am, in Jesus name.
4. I want to pay more tithes and offerings, therefore give me the opportunity, in Jesus name.
5. I want to be a financial pillar in your house, therefore my Lord increase my income, in Jesus name.
6. Father Lord, promotion is a sign that my Lord is with me, therefore show others that you are with me, in Jesus name.
7. I want a better life for my family therefore move me to a higher level, in Jesus name.
8. Father Lord, I want to be a financial blessing to others, therefore give me increase, in Jesus name.
9. Heavenly father, give me increase as a favor from you O' Lord, in Jesus name.

10. Increase is a sign of your presence in the lives of your children; therefore give me increase O' Lord, so I can demonstrate your presence in my life, in Jesus name.

11. Father Lord, let my business yield profit, in Jesus name.

12. Your word says the profit of the land is for all; therefore give me my share of this land, in Jesus name (Ecclesiastes 5:9).

13. Your word says you will rain on my land to yield increase, so father bless what I do, so I can experience increase, in Jesus name (Lev 26:4).

14. If I am willing and obedient, I shall eat the good of the land; therefore help me to be obedient, because I am willing O' Lord, in Jesus name.

15. Father Lord, remove obstacles that are standing against my promotion, in Jesus name.

16. Almighty father, let me disassociate from people who will not let me move forward, in Jesus name.

17. Father Lord, help me silence voices that would not let me take the steps I need to move forward, in Jesus name.

18. Father Lord, help me make the right choices that would lead to my promotion, in Jesus name.

19. Father Lord, help me see your instructions for me to move forward, in Jesus name

20. Father Lord, you said you are the one who teaches me to profit, therefore teach me how to profit, my Lord, in Jesus name (Isaiah 48:17).

21. Father Lord, you say you would show me the way to go; father show me the way to go to get profit, in Jesus name (Isaiah 48:17).

22. Father Lord, help me hear your instructions on how to get increase in my business, in Jesus name.

23. Almighty father, send needed helpers to me that will push me beyond my efforts, in Jesus name.

24. O' Lord take me to a location of your calling for my life, in Jesus name.

25. Father Lord, scatter every gathering against my progress, in Jesus name.

26. Father Lord, help me to obey you so that your blessings would overtake me, in Jesus name.

27. Father Lord, bless me with your blessings; for your blessings give increase and brings no sorrow with it, in Jesus name.

28. Heavenly father, bless me indeed and enlarge my territory, in Jesus name.

29. Father Lord, open the windows of heaven and pour me blessings, which I shall not have room to receive, in Jesus name.

30. Father Lord, help me to be a lender and not a debtor, in Jesus name.

31. Father Lord, raise me up, so I can raise your name higher, in Jesus name.

32. Father Lord, destroy anything in my foundation that may hold me back, in Jesus name.

33. O' Lord remove powers in me that might be refusing me from getting desired promotion and increase, in Jesus name.

34. Father, Lord, please promote those you know are due for promotion, in Jesus name.

35. Father, please break every chain that has held your children bound from receiving their due promotions, in Jesus name.

CHAPTER 12

HOUSEHOLD ENEMIES

"A man's foes shall be members of his own Household".
–Matthew 10:36.

1. Father Lord, save me from powers of my household, in Jesus name."
2. Heavenly father, paralyze powers within my reach that stand against me, in Jesus name.
3. Almighty father, please expose powers within my household that are against me, in Jesus name.
4. O' Lord, help me tread upon serpents and scorpions within my family & friends, in Jesus name.
5. Father, please protect my mouth from divulging my secret to the household wickedness, in Jesus name.
6. Father, please help me nullify the effectiveness of my enemies within my reach, in Jesus name.
7. Almighty father, raise me up above the reach of my household enemies, in Jesus name.
8. Almighty God, help me trample upon my household enemies, in Jesus name.
9. Father, Lord, please expose, so I can avoid my household enemies, in Jesus name.
10. Almighty father, help me close the access I have given to my household enemies, in Jesus name.
11. Oh Lord raise me higher than the reach of my household enemies, in Jesus name.

12. My father, turn against them handshake of evil, in Jesus name.
13. My God let no hand of failure within my family touch me, in Jesus name.
14. Every handwriting of failure written in my family be erased, in Jesus name.
15. Father, let those touching me with evil hands have no evil effect on me, in Jesus name.
16. Father, bless those who are blessing me and curse those who are cursing me, in Jesus name.
17. Father, keep your eyes upon me as the apple of your eyes, in Jesus name.
18. Father, encompass me with your righteous hands always, in Jesus name.
19. Oh Lord, keep me as the head, on top, and never the tail or below, in Jesus name.
20. Father, let those eating and drinking with me never able to plan evil against me, in Jesus name.
21. Father, scatter those who gather against me, in Jesus name.
22. Father, destroy the desires of my household enemies, in the name of Jesus.
23. Father, strengthen me and let not my household enemies put me to shame, in Jesus name.
24. My Lord, do not put me to shame before my household enemies, in Jesus name.
25. Father, lift me up despite those pulling me down within my friends and family members, in Jesus name.
26. Father, uproot evil family tree in my family, in Jesus name.
27. Father, remove me from family bondages, in Jesus name.
28. Heavenly father, distance me from family failures, in Jesus name.

29. Father, remove me from common prison of my family, in Jesus name.
30. Father, turn my enemies' joy to sorrow, in Jesus name.
31. Father, distance me from the failures of those who were before me in this family, in the name of Jesus.
32. Father, release me from the control and influence of my household enemies, in Jesus name.
33. Father, free me from household evil ties, in Jesus name.
34. Father, help me to stand firmly on the liberty of your freedom in Jesus name.
35. Father, keep me free indeed according to your word, in Jesus name.

CHAPTER 13

STAGNATION

"You have circled this mountain long enough turn and go northward". –Deuteronomy 2:3.

1. Father, I surrender myself to you that you move me forward, in Jesus name.
2. Heavenly father, remove me from satanic captivity, in Jesus name.
3. Father, help me break down powers that kept me in one place, in Jesus name.
4. Father, help me escape the devil's trap, in Jesus name.
5. Father, move me away from snail progress and shoot me up by your power, in Jesus name.
6. Father, remove me from the seat of stagnation, in Jesus name.
7. Heavenly father, please remove me from my comfortable seat, so I can move forward, in Jesus name.
8. Every spirit of stagnation that is set against me must leave me now, in Jesus mighty name.
9. I break the power of stagnation over me, in Jesus name.
10. Father, release me from every cage that keeps me in stagnation, in Jesus name.
11. I refuse to be kept in one place, in Jesus name.
12. O' Lord distance me from family stagnation powers, in Jesus name.
13. Father, move me forward, so my testimony brings glory to your name, in Jesus name.

14. Father, let the blood of Jesus wash away every slippery situation that refuses me from climbing higher, in the mighty name of Jesus.
15. Father, remove me from the valley of stagnation and help me climb the mountain of your grace, in Jesus mighty name.
16. Father, let the angels of the Lord help me move forward, in Jesus name.
17. Almighty father, whatever is in me that refuses progress, take it away from me, in Jesus name.
18. O' Lord break my ties with any and every association that keeps me in one position, in Jesus mighty name.
19. Father, help me reach my destiny, in Jesus name.
20. Father, help me be a blessing to those who are depending on me, in Jesus name.
21. Father, help me take my place as a leader, so I can lead my people, in Jesus name.
22. Father, break me away from evil kingdom reigning in my life, in Jesus name.
23. Father, disgrace evil stagnation spirit assigned to keep me down, in Jesus name.
24. Father Lord, establish me to carry forward your cross, in Jesus name.
25. Father Lord, bless me, so I can be a financial pillar for your work, in Jesus name.
26. Father, I am more than a conqueror; therefore help me begin to conquer powers that are holding me down, in the mighty name of Jesus.
27. Father, forgive me of every sin that might keep me in stagnation, in Jesus name.
28. Father stand around me, so I can stand and move forward for you, in Jesus name.
29. Father, blow your wind of progress into my life, so I can move forward, in Jesus name.

30. Father Lord, settle me where you know I can prosper, in the name of Jesus Christ.

31. Father, help me break every curse that may have kept me stagnant, in Jesus mighty name.

32. Father, deliver me from every inherited stagnancy, in the name of Jesus Christ.

33. Father, deliver me from dependency that may have kept me stagnant, in Jesus name.

34. Every wall that blocked me from moving forward is destroyed, in Jesus name.

35. Those not pulling their weights that have kept your church stagnant; strengthen them O' Lord to begin doing their parts, in Jesus name.

36. Let every member of the church take his or her place so the work begin to move forward, in Jesus name.

37. Let me do my part, so that the group will begin achieving more, in Jesus name.

38. O' Lord, give us new ideas that will move us forward, in Jesus name.

39. Heavenly Lord, let our Divine helpers come quickly, so we can move forward, in Jesus name.

40. Let the Divine helpers of my children and my siblings locate them to move them forward, in Jesus name.

CHAPTER 14

BURDENED HEART

"Come to me all you who labor and heaven laden and I will give you rest". –Matthew 11:28.

"Cast your burden on the Lord and He will sustain you and he will never permit the righteous to be moved". –Psalm 55:22.

1. My heart is burdened and I need your help, O' Lord, help me, in Jesus name.
2. Father Lord, help me remove every burden I now carry, in Jesus name.
3. Almighty father, help me return evil load I carry to the owners, in Jesus name.
4. Heavenly father, release me from a life of worry, in Jesus name.
5. Father, help me to lean on you O' Lord more than ever before, in Jesus name.
6. Father Lord, increase my faith in you, so I can release my burdens on you, in Jesus name.
7. Father, release me from association that brings me worry, in Jesus name.
8. O' Lord, help me overcome fear that cause burdens on my heart, in Jesus name.
9. Father deliver me from voices, both inside and outside that keep me burdened, in Jesus name.

10. Almighty God, help me put my past in my past, in Jesus name.

11. Father Lord, help me put in its place every experience that keeps me burdened, in Jesus name.

12. Father, free my heart to receive your Holy Spirit, in Jesus name.

13. Father Lord, clean my spirit, so you can dwell in me as your temple forever, in Jesus name.

14. Heavenly father, sweep my heart from impurities deposited, in me in Jesus name.

15. Almighty God, help me know that tomorrow belongs to you, in Jesus name.

16. Father Lord, deliver me from the spirit of depression that keeps me burdened, in Jesus mighty name.

17. Father Lord, release my caged happiness and joy, in the Jesus mighty name.

18. Father, please release me from any caged soul in Jesus name.

19. Spirit of confusion operating within me, depart now, in Jesus name.

20. Every elements of confusion around me I command you to leave now, in Jesus name.

21. I am a salt on the earth and I shall not lose my saltiness, in Jesus name.

22. I am a light that cannot be hidden upon the earth, father, let me begin to shine, in Jesus name.

23. Father Lord, let my season of worry come to an end now, in Jesus name.

24. Heavenly father, wherever I go to pick up worry, help me to avoid the place, in Jesus name.

25. Almighty God, the power over me that cause me to worry, father put that power under me, in Jesus mighty name.

26. Every shadow of fear that causes me to worry, father Lord, help me erase the shadow, in Jesus name.

27. Whatever draws me to where to pick up worry, father deliver me from that place, in Jesus name.

28. Father Lord, silence what I hear that cause me to worry, in Jesus name.

29. Heavenly father, free me from debt that could cause me to worry, in Jesus name.

30. Almighty father, help me pay off my debts, in Jesus name.

31. Heavenly father, help me not to live above my means, in Jesus name.

32. Almighty God, stabilize my joy in Jesus name.

33. Father Lord, free me from the roller-coastal of happiness, in Jesus name.

34. Father Lord, help my mood to see things the way you see them, in Jesus name.

35. Almighty God, close doors and windows that bring me fears, in Jesus name.

36. Father, help me focus on what I have and not on the things I do not have, in Jesus name.

37. Father, help me remember prayers you have answered for me and not the ones you are yet to answer, in Jesus name.

CHAPTER 15

OPEN HEAVEN

Try me if I will not open to you the windows of heaven and pour out for you such blessing that there will not be room enough to receive it. –Malachi 3:10.

"The Lord will open unto you His good treasure and the heaven will give rain unto your land in its season and to bless all the works of your hand and you shall lend unto many nations and you shall not borrow". –Deuteronomy 28: 12:"

1. Father Lord, open your Heaven to me and let me enjoy your resources, in Jesus name.
2. Heavenly father, only you can turn things around in a day, therefore turn my situation around, in Jesus name.
3. Father Lord, I look only to you; therefore bless me from your heavenly resources, in Jesus name.
4. Father Lord, prepare me for heavenly blessings, in Jesus name.
5. Father Lord, draw me closer to yourself, so I can enjoy your heavenly resources, in Jesus name.
6. Almighty father, help me to begin enjoying the goodness of your heaven, in Jesus name.
7. Father Lord, let your spiritual blessings manifest in my life, in Jesus name.
8. Father Lord, place me in a location where heavenly resources will locate me quickly, in Jesus name.

9. My Lord, open my eyes to see where to be, so I would begin to enjoy your heavenly treasures, in Jesus name.

10. O' Lord, help me to always be at the right place at the right time to receive your heavenly blessings, in Jesus name.

11. Father Lord, help me to hear from you on where to be on a daily basis, in Jesus name.

12. Father Lord, let heaven open to receive my tithes and offerings, in Jesus name.

13. Father Lord, help me do what I need to do, so that heaven will respond to me, in Jesus name.

14. Heavenly father, help me put in my best, so that I can receive the best of heaven, in Jesus name.

15. Almighty father, let heaven open for you to hear all of my supplications, in Jesus name.

16. Father Lord, teach me what to say at any time to you, in Jesus name.

17. Father Lord, let heaven comfort me the day I go through a tough time, in Jesus name.

18. O' Lord give me a word from you daily to go through my daily activities, in Jesus name.

19. Every evil covenant I may have entered without knowing the consequences, please help me break them, in Jesus name.

20. Almighty father, let heaven reject programs by the enemy against me, in Jesus name.

21. Father Lord, let heaven reject every ill judgment against me, in Jesus name.

22. Father Lord, let your heavenly glory locate my star, in Jesus name.

23. Father Lord, let my star be invincible to read by those who have ill intentions against me, in Jesus name.

24. My Lord, let heaven blind those searching for my star to do me harm, in Jesus name.

25. Father Lord, let heaven release the light I need into my night and the cloud I need into my day for my productive days and nights, in Jesus mighty name.

26. Father Lord, every rearrangement of my stars by the wicked powers should be canceled, in Jesus name.

27. Father Lord, frustrate those searching the heavens to locate my whereabouts, in Jesus name.

28. Father Lord, let heaven waste efforts of my enemies against me, in Jesus name.

29. Father Lord, let the enchantments to heaven by my enemies return null and void, in Jesus name.

30. Father, let this day, month, this year become of harvest for me, in Jesus name.

31. Father Lord, turn my luck around, so that I become a lender and not a borrower, in Jesus name.

32. Father Lord, let heavenly power give me strength, so that no one can intimidate me, in Jesus name.

33. Almighty father, let heaven break bondages laid ahead of me, in Jesus name.

34. Father Lord, let heavenly wisdom locate me, so I do not fall prey to cheap tricks of Satan, in Jesus name.

35. Father Lord, nullify every program of failure against me, in Jesus name.

36. Every evil waiting for a trigger date, I command you to expire now, in Jesus name.

CHAPTER 16

FEAR

"For God has not given us the spirit of fear, but of power, of love and of a sound mind". -2Timothy 1:7.

1. Father Lord, fear is not of you and not from you; therefore help me to overcome fear, in Jesus name.
2. Every spirit of fear living with me that wants to rob me of my faith; please help me to overcome the power, in Jesus name.
3. I break the power of fear constantly on my spirit, in the name of Jesus.
4. Every stronghold of fear in my life, I destroy you with the name of Jesus, in Jesus name.
5. For I know you hold my tomorrow, therefore free me from the fear of tomorrow, in Jesus name.
6. Father Lord, help me break any stronghold of fear, in Jesus name.
7. Heavenly father, send my fears back to where it came from, in Jesus name.
8. My Lord, lead me away from what brings me fear, in Jesus name.
9. Heavenly father, distance me from the fear always on my mind, in Jesus name.
10. Father Lord, let me overcome my Goliath and use him as a stepping stone, in Jesus name.
11. Father Lord, help me overcome my fears of today, in Jesus mighty name.

12. Heavenly father, help me overcome fears for drunk drivers, in Jesus name.

13. Father, help me erase my fears of an accident, in Jesus name.

14. Father Lord, help me overcome fears that I cannot explain why I am afraid, in Jesus name.

15. Heavenly father take away my fear of diseases that are killing others, in Jesus name.

16. Almighty God, help me to know that I am under your shadows that thousands shall fall on my side, but it shall not come near me, in Jesus name.

17. Father Lord, help me overcome the fear of poverty and lack, in Jesus name.

18. I erase things that make me afraid of darkness, in Jesus name.

19. Whatever makes me afraid at night time, father, help me overcome it, in Jesus mighty name.

20. Father, give me your word at the right time to overcome whatever would cause fear in my day, in Jesus name.

21. I silence voices that make me easily afraid, in Jesus name.

22. Father, renew my mind to look at only the good in everything and not the negative side of things, in Jesus name.

23. I prophesy into my day that I am more than a conqueror everywhere I go in Jesus name.

24. I overcome you fear of failure, in Jesus name.

25. I overcome constantly worrying that someone would do evil to me, in Jesus name.

26. I overcome you, you fear that people are ganging up against me, in Jesus name.

27. I erase the fear that my application will be denied, in Jesus name.

28. Father Lord, help me erase the fear that my efforts would be wasted, in Jesus name.

29. Father Lord, help me overcome the fear that I will not succeed, in Jesus name.
30. Father Lord, help me win the war in my head, in Jesus name.
31. Father Lord, help me erase the fear that something bad would happen to me, in Jesus name.
32. The failure of others is not my portion, in Jesus name.
33. I erase the fear of what happened to my friends who tried and failed, in Jesus name.
34. Father, help me destroy powers waiting to make me afraid, in Jesus name.
35. Father Lord, detach me from inherited fear, in Jesus name.
36. I overcome the fear of anything created by God, in Jesus name.
37. Let fear be a thing of the past in the lives of my children, in Jesus name.
38. Help us define fear as False Evidence Appearing Real daily, in Jesus name.
39. Help us to be calculative and not fear of taking risks, in Jesus name.
40. Let those with the voice of fear be distant from our church, in Jesus name.

CHAPTER 17

SHAME AND REPROACH

"You know my reproach, my shame, and my dishonor; my adversaries are all before you." –Psalm 69:19.

1. Whatever I have done in the past, please let me not destroy myself in the shame, in Jesus name.
2. Father Lord, help me to look to my future and leave my past to the past, in Jesus name.
3. Father Lord, let no voice in me bring me down, because of my past reproaches and shame, in Jesus name.
4. Father Lord help me to know that my past belongs to my past, in Jesus name.
5. Heavenly father, please help me shut doors my past deeds would open to me, in Jesus name.
6. Almighty father, I am new in Christ and help me to live the rest of my life as a new man, in Jesus name.
7. Heavenly father, help me not to make new friends that would remind of me of my past, in Jesus name.
8. O' Lord, seal and throw away my past, in the name of Jesus.
9. My father, my father, help me not to dwell in the goodness of my past, in Jesus name.
10. My Lord, help me not to dwell in the bad things that happened to me in the past, in Jesus name.
11. Father Lord, I know a lot of my enemies want to see me put to shame, do not put me to shame, in Jesus name.

12. Father, I lean on your word and let your word be the overcoming power I need to overcome shame, in Jesus name.

13. Almighty God, help me defeat every satanic agent assigned to put me to shame, in Jesus name.

14. O' Lord help me shut every door I have opened to the enemy that would put me to shame, in Jesus name.

15. Almighty father, help me overcome the urge of anger that would put me to shame, in Jesus name.

16. O' Lord, help me overcome the urge of lust that would put me to shame, in Jesus name.

17. Father, help me conquer any urge in me that would put me to shame, in Jesus name.

18. Father, help me eliminate the sin that would disgrace me, in Jesus name.

19. Father, help me shut every door of shame I am opening to the enemy, in Jesus name.

20. Spirit of failure, I bound you from putting me to shame, in Jesus name.

21. Father, help me to be a slave to righteousness, so shame shall have no place in me, in Jesus name.

22. Father Lord, open my eyes, so I will not do the things that would put me to shame, in Jesus name.

23. Father Lord, send your angel to drag me away from doing things that would bring shame to me and my family, in Jesus name.

24. Whatever has brought shame to my family in the past let me be far from it, in Jesus name.

25. Father Lord, distance me from temptations that would expose me to shame, in Jesus name.

26. Father Lord, help me to remain the head and not the tail where I would experience shame, in Jesus name.

27. I bind and cast out every perverted spirit that would disgrace me, in Jesus name.

28. I bind and cast out every spirit of perverted lifestyle, in Jesus name.
29. Holy Lord, pour your Holy Spirit in me, so I would avoid perverted mind, in Jesus name.
30. I bind and cast out the spirit that leads many to a shameful end, in Jesus name.
31. I shall end whatever I do in glory, I ask in Jesus name.
32. I shall not finish whatever I do in shame, in Jesus name.
33. Shame is not my portion, in Jesus name.
34. Father Lord, help me remove every garment of shame, in Jesus name.
35. Father Lord, put on me your garment of praise, in Jesus name.
36. My wife shall not bring shame to our household, in Jesus name.
37. My children shall not experience shame, in Jesus name.
38. My husband shall not be put to shame, in Jesus name.
39. I shall not be an agent of shame, in Jesus name.
40. Father Lord, erase marks of shame from my life, in Jesus name.

CHAPTER 18

DELIVERANCE

"And God sent me before you to preserve a posterity for you in the earth, and to save your lives by a great deliverance". –Genesis 45:7.

1. Father Lord, I need my posterity on the earth, therefore deliver me from powers of darkness, in Jesus name.
2. Father Lord, Help me live like one redeemed of the Lord, in Jesus name.
3. Heavenly father, help me to stand in the liberty of your deliverance, in Jesus name.
4. Father, deliver me from ancestral curses, in Jesus name.
5. Father Lord, help me to overcome family bondages, in Jesus name.
6. Every chain of sorrow break from me now, in Jesus name.
7. Evil family tree, be uprooted from my life, in Jesus name.
8. Father Lord, I am free from the sin of my forefathers, in Jesus name.
9. Father Lord, deliver me from spiritual blindness, in Jesus name.
10. Heavenly father, remove every veil that refuse to let me see the path of my success, in Jesus name.
11. Father Lord, open my ears to hear your instruction for success, in Jesus name.
12. Father, deliver me from spiritual deafness, in Jesus name.

13. Father, deliver me from being at the wrong place at the wrong time, in Jesus name.
14. Father, deliver me from every strongman assigned to wrestle with my destiny, in Jesus name.
15. Father Lord, consume away powers that would keep me stagnant, in Jesus name.
16. Father Lord, remove me from confusion, in Jesus name.
17. Father Lord, remove every spirit of confusion from me, in Jesus name.
18. Your word promised to break every yoke on my neck, so it shall be for me, in Jesus name (Isaiah 10:27).
19. My shoulders shall respond to you as you remove every burden from it, in Jesus name.
20. Father, deliver me from evil prayers, in Jesus name.
21. Father Lord, help me to overcome every evil laying of hands by Pastors and priests, in Jesus name.
22. Father Lord, help me overcome the powers from evil altars erected for me, in Jesus name.
23. Father Lord, divert to my enemies every enchantment of evil from evil altars against me, in Jesus name.
24. Father Lord, deliver me from evil monitors, in Jesus name.
25. Father, Lift me up, so I would be too high up to be pulled down, in Jesus name.
26. Father Lord, expose and show me a way of escape from evil manipulations, in Jesus name.
27. Father, deliver me from marine powers, in Jesus name.
28. O' Lord deliver me from powers using your creations against me, in Jesus name.
29. Heavenly father, deprogram every negative programming against me in the atmosphere in Jesus name.
30. O' Lord let your creations begin to favor me and anything of interest to me, in Jesus name.

31. Father, deliver me from those reading and attacking my star, in Jesus name.

32. O' Lord blow away every blur on my star, in Jesus name.

33. Father Lord, erase every mark of the devil on me, in Jesus name.

34. I revoke every embargo of failure on me, in Jesus name.

35. I cancel every chain meant to hold me or any member of my family, in Jesus name.

36. Father, deliver me and my household from spiritual wickedness, in Jesus name.

37. Father thank you for making me and my family more than conquerors, in Jesus name.

38. Father, deliver us from inherited sickness, illness, and diseases, in Jesus mighty name.

39. My father, my father, exempt me from territorial limitations, in Jesus name.

40. Heavenly father, deliver me from those who want to quench my fire, in Jesus name.

CHAPTER 19

BINDING AND CASTING AWAY

"Most assuredly, I say to you, whatever you bind on earth will be bound in heaven, and whatever you loose on earth will be loosed in heaven". –Matthew 18:18.

"I will give you the keys to the kingdom of God that whatsoever you bound on earth shall be bound in heaven and whatever you loose on earth shall be loosen in heaven". -Matthew 16: 19.

1. Father Lord, help me believe that what I bind shall remain bound, in Jesus name.
2. Father Lord, help me to believe that what I loose shall be loosen, in Jesus name.
3. Father Lord, help me to remember that binding and loosening is an authority that I already have, in Jesus name.
4. Heavenly father, I bind and cast out the spirit of unbelief, in Jesus name.
5. Almighty God, teach me areas I should not put up with, in Jesus name.
6. O' Lord I bind the spirit of failure, in Jesus name.
7. Heavenly father, I bind and cast away any spirit of sickness, illness and diseases, in Jesus name.
8. Father Lord, release the spirit of happiness and joy in my life, in Jesus name

9. Heaven father, loose the spirit of favor, in my life and the life of my family, in Jesus name.

10. Father Lord, I bind and cast out any spirit that would keep me in one place, in Jesus name.

11. I bind and cast out any spirit that will keep me in chains, in Jesus mighty name.

12. Heavenly father, I bind and cast out any spirit that would lure me into temptation, in Jesus name.

13. Almighty father, I bind and cast away spirit of procrastination, in Jesus name.

14. I bind and cast out the spirit of lust, in Jesus name.

15. I bind and cast away any spirit of poverty, in Jesus name.

16. I bind and cast out spirit of disappointment, in Jesus name.

17. I bind and cast out every spirit of inherited failure, in Jesus name.

18. I bind and cast out the spirit that held my father and mother captive, in Jesus name.

19. I bind and cast out spirit of common prison, in my father's house and my mother's house, in Jesus name.

20. Father Lord, I bind and cast out spirit of lack, in Jesus name.

21. I bind and cast away shame, in Jesus name.

22. I bind and cast away unfriendly friends, in Jesus name.

23. I loosen the spirit of abundance of good thing in to my home, in Jesus name.

24. I loosen prosperity in my life, in Jesus name.

25. I loosen greatness into my life, in Jesus name.

26. I loosen forgiving spirit into my life, in Jesus name.

27. I bind every spirit of un-forgiveness, in Jesus name.

28. I loosen the spirit of giving and receiving into my life, in Jesus name.

29. I loosen the spirit of obedience to God into my life, in Jesus name.

30. I loosen the spirit of favor into my life and the life of my wife and my children, in Jesus name.

31. I loosen the spirit of accelerated progress into my life, in Jesus name.

32. I loosen the spirit of friendship and hospitality into my life, in Jesus name.

33. I bind and cast away spirit of depression, in Jesus name.

34. Spirit of loneliness I bind you and cast you out now, in Jesus name.

35. I bind and cast out spirit of sudden death, in Jesus name.

36. Spirit of starting and completion come and dwell with me now, in Jesus name.

37. I bind the spirit of high blood pressure from me and my family members, in Jesus name.

38. I bind powers strangulating my labor in this city and this country, in Jesus name.

39. I bind and cast out those empowering spirits of failure in our lives, in Jesus name.

40. Let powers of incompleteness seize from all of our endeavors, in Jesus name.

CHAPTER 20

ANOINTING

Anointing is the power of God, which can separate you and what you do from your competition. When God anoints you for what you do, you will excel, even if you hide under the ground, customers and patrons would find you and that is why we need to pray for God to anoint us and what we do.

"How God anointed Jesus of Nazareth with the Holy Spirit and with power, who went about doing good and healing all who were oppressed by the devil, for God was with Him." –Acts 10:38.

1. O Lord my father, I understand the power of anointing, so anoint me for life, in Jesus name.
2. Heavenly father, wherever I am, let your anointing separate me for yourself, in Jesus name.
3. Father, let the power of your anointing lead me into my calling, in Jesus name.
4. Father, anoint my eyes to see where you are leading me, in Jesus name.
5. Almighty God, anoint my ears to hear what you are saying, in Jesus name.
6. Father Lord, let your anointing separate me for prosperity in all that I do, in Jesus name.
7. Almighty God, let the power of your anointing grant me more of your favor, in Jesus name.

8. Father, let your anointing announce me to the world, in Jesus name.

9. Father, let your anointing announce my business to the world, in Jesus name.

10. Father, anoint me that even when I am in error, it will not be pronounce, in Jesus name.

11. Father, anoint me so that even in bad times, my investment would yield great returns, in Jesus name.

12. Oh Lord, anoint me that whatever my fingers touch produce a good harvest, in Jesus name

CHAPTER 21

WINDS OF GOD

"Against Elam I will bring the four winds from the four quarters of heaven and scatter them toward all those winds; there shall be no nations where the outcast of Elam will not go" – Jeremiah 49:36.

1. East wind of God come and blow away all my afflictions, in Jesus name.
2. North wind, bring me promotions, in Jesus name.
3. Whatever the enemy has prepared against me, father Lord, let your wind blow it away, in Jesus name I ask.
4. Father Lord, let your wind bring me the peace I need, in Jesus name.
5. Let your east wind O' Lord remove deafness in me, in Jesus name.
6. Every raging storm in my life let the wind of
   a. God calm the storms down, in Jesus name.
7. Father Lord, let your east wind blow away every war the enemies have waged against me, in Jesus name.
8. Every wall erected to stop me, let the east wind of God blow the wall down, in Jesus name.
9. Let the east wind take away every locust in my life to eat my blessings, in Jesus name.
10. I ask the wind that brought Israelites quail to bring me my meat from far and near, in Jesus name.
11. Father Lord, help me to fly spiritually riding on the wings of the cherubs, in Jesus name.

12. Father Lord, let your wind bring me the desired rain of blessing, in Jesus name.
13. Father, let your winds tear apart every mountain that confront me, in Jesus name.
14. Let the wind of God break into pieces every rock that obstruct me, in Jesus name.
15. Father Lord, be in every wind that blows my way, in Jesus name.
16. Father Lord, let the wind that would bring me rain be invincible to my enemies, in Jesus name.
17. Let the water that your wind brings to me be enough to satisfy me and my household, in Jesus name.
18. Let the wind of God blow and collapse the building where my enemies are gathered, in Jesus name.
19. Father let the words of my mouth bring my prayers to you with the help of your wind, in Jesus name.
20. My Father, my father let your wind blow my problems away like chaff, in Jesus name.
21. Father, let your east wind carry me out of where I am not supposed to be, in Jesus name.
22. When my enemies come looking for me, let me escape riding on your wind, in Jesus name.
23. Father Lord, let your south wind bring peace to this country and the world, in Jesus name.
24. O' Lord my father, let your wind clear out every fog in my sight, in Jesus name.
25. Let your wind scatter every evil thought that might come to my mind, in Jesus name.
26. Father, let your wind help me beat small all the enemies of my progress, in Jesus name.
27. Father Lord, let your wind break into pieces the boat of poverty I am riding on, in Jesus name.
28. Heavenly Father, let your wind break the boat of lack I am riding on, in Jesus name.

29. Father let your wind blow away my sorrow that it does not happen again, in Jesus name.

30. Let your wind O' Lord help me withstand every storm I would ever pass through, in Jesus name.

31. Father Lord, let your wind cause every door of blessing that are closed against me to be reopened. I ask in Jesus name.

32. Father Lord, let me not labor for the wind, in Jesus name.

33. Father Lord, let no evil wind distract my timings, in Jesus name.

34. Father Lord, let your north and south winds blow on my ventures, so that I will reap abundance. In Jesus name, I ask.

35. Father Lord, let your wind bring me rain while I am in the wilderness, in Jesus name.

CHAPTER 22

FORGIVENESS

"If we say have no sin, we deceive ourselves and the truth is not in us, but if we confess our sins, He is faithful and just to forgive all of our sins and He will cleanse us from all unrighteousness" -1 John 8: 8 – 9:.

1. Father Lord, please forgive all of my sins; both intentional and unintentional sins, in Jesus name.
2. Father Lord, please wash away my sins of thoughts, in Jesus name.
3. father every sin through my evil actions, please forgive me, in Jesus name.
4. Father Lord, please forgive me of every sin of inaction, in Jesus name.
5. Father Lord, please forgive me of joint sins with others, in Jesus name.
6. Father, please forgive me of sins of my household in Jesus name.
7. Heavenly father, please forgive me of sins by association, in Jesus name.
8. My Lord, please forgive me of the sins of disassociation, in Jesus name.
9. Heavenly father, please forgive me of sins of disobedience, in Jesus name.
10. O' Lord, please forgive me of sins I have committed by lack of faith in you, in Jesus name.

11. Heavenly father, please forgive me of all sins pertaining to my past relationships, in Jesus name.

12. Almighty God, please forgive me of sins of fornication and adulterous intentions and actions, in Jesus name.

13. Heavenly father, please forgive me of sins out of lying and pervasive actions, in Jesus name.

14. O' Lord, please forgive me of sins out of wicked actions or wicked inactions, in Jesus name.

15. Heavenly father, please forgive me of sins meant to pay back evil done to me, in Jesus name.

16. Father Lord, please forgive me of sins out of repayment to others, in Jesus name.

17. Heavenly father, please forgive me for not remembering someone who wronged me that I should forgive, in Jesus name.

18. My Lord, please forgive me for having held grudges against those who were unjust to me in the past that I cannot remember who they are, in Jesus name.

19. Father Lord, please forgive me of sins I committed out of youthful deeds, in Jesus name.

20. Heavenly father, please forgive me of the sins I committed against my father, in Jesus name.

21. Heavenly father, please forgive me of the sins I committed against my mother, in Jesus name.

22. Father, please forgive me of sins I committed against my grandparents, in Jesus name.

23. Father Lord, please forgive me of sins I committed against the Holy Spirit, in Jesus name.

24. Almighty father, please forgive me of sins I committed to deny Jesus Christ in the past, in Jesus name.

25. Father Lord, please forgive me of sins I committed against my city, State, and nation, in Jesus name.

26. Heavenly father, please forgive me of sins I committed against rulers of my city, state, and country, in Jesus name.
27. My Lord, please forgive me of sins I committed to strangers, in Jesus name.
28. My Father in heaven, please forgive me of sins I committed to my own people, in Jesus name.
29. My Lord, please forgive me of sins I committed against people who trusted me, in Jesus name.
30. Father Lord, please forgive me of sins I committed against the ground and the atmosphere, in Jesus name.
31. Heavenly father, please forgive me of any sins I committed against any heavenly bodies, in Jesus name.
32. Almighty God, please forgive me of sins I committed against any of your creation, in Jesus name.

CHAPTER 23

PRAYER FOR THE NATION

"If my people which are called by my name will humble themselves and pray and seek my face, and turn from their wicked ways, then will I hear from heaven and forgive their sins and heal their land."- 2 Chronicles 7:14.

1. Father Lord, let the hearts of the people of our land humble themselves, in Jesus name.
2. You permitted this country to be formed, do not turn away from us now, in Jesus name.
3. We bind all principalities and powers that have dominion in this country, in Jesus name.
4. Father, release your power of God to operate freely in this country, in the name of Jesus.
5. I pray against powers of darkness operating freely, in this country in Jesus name.
6. Father, forgive all of us for the past and present evil deeds, in Jesus name.
7. Father, cause repentance to come upon this country, in Jesus name.
8. Father, let the churches have power that will turn the hearts of many to you, in Jesus name.
9. Father, I pray for your revival to come down on your church and all the people, in Jesus name.
10. Let your men and women of God stand up to defend their faith, in Jesus name.
11. Let your spirit be seen in all of us, in Jesus name.

12. Father, release your power on us, in Jesus name.
13. Father, stir up the country, so they know to run to you alone, in Jesus name.
14. Father, I pray that you do not take your mercies away from us, in Jesus name.
15. Let the land be healed of the sickness or diseases that are prevalent, in Jesus name.
16. Bend the hearts of the rulers toward you O'
    b. Lord, in Jesus name.
17. Let the Goliaths of our country fail, in Jesus name
18. I paralyze all powers confronting my country, in Jesus name.
19. Father, help us to eliminate the sin that is about to bring down my country, in Jesus name.
20. Let the powers influencing sin in my country be destroyed by fire, in Jesus name.
21. Let every enemy of my country be rendered impotent, in Jesus name.
22. Every gathering by others to destroy my country face the resistance of God, in Jesus name.
23. Every evil plan against the financial dept of my country catches fire now, in Jesus name.
24. Evil plan against the leaders of my country be destroyed, in Jesus name.
25. Every territorial power opposing the progress of my country is hereby destroyed, in Jesus name.
26. Father, usher in a new dawn for my country, in Jesus mighty name.
27. Every condemnation assigned against my country is reversed, in Jesus mighty name.
28. Heavenly father, all foundational problems confronting my country are canceled, in Jesus name.

29. Every idol existing in the location of my country before its beginning shall become dormant and die, in Jesus mighty name.

30. Every power rising from the sea against my country is stopped, in Jesus name.

31. Every unfriendly allies of my country are hereby exposed for what they are, in Jesus name.

32. Father, come and take your place as the head, the Elohim of our lives, in Jesus name.

33. Father help us defeat every unseen battles waged against my country, in Jesus name.

34. Father Lord, destroy the walls against progress erected by the evil ones, in Jesus name.

35. Father Lord, help us eliminate poverty, in Jesus name.

36. Let witchcraft activities in this country be confronted by the Spirit of God, in Jesus name.

37. Father Lord, send down consuming fire against secret societies in my country, in Jesus name.

38. Father set fire against demonic altars having their ways with my country, in Jesus name.

39. Father Lord, release your Spirit over my country, in Jesus name.

40. Father Lord, let my country ally with progressive countries toward you O' Lord, in Jesus name.

CHAPTER 24

POWER OF GOD

"Look to me, and be saved, all you ends of the earth, for I am God, and there is no other." -Isaiah 45:22.

1. Father Lord, I look unto you and unto you alone, help me to keep my focus on you, in Jesus name.
2. Heavenly father, from you all my help comes, therefore let nothing in me stops you from sending your help to me, in Jesus name.
3. Father Lord, you opened the sea for the Israelites to go through, therefore open every Red sea holding me back, so I can cross into my promise land, in Jesus name.
4. Father Lord, use your power to change my name like you did to Jacob, in Jesus name.
5. Father Lord, use your power to move me out of captivity holding me, in Jesus name.
6. Father by your power put in my mouth words that would prosper me, in Jesus name.
7. Heavenly father, put in the mouths of my enemies words that would bless me, in Jesus name.
8. Father Lord, by your power give me the power to get wealth, in Jesus name.
9. By your power O' Lord, perfect all that concerns me, in Jesus name.
10. By your power, O' Lord, let my enemies not prevail against me, in Jesus name.

11. Father, by your power, send me help even when it seems impossible to help me, in Jesus name.
12. My father, my father, let no one stand against your help for me, O' Lord, in Jesus name.
13. By your mighty hand let my enemies fall before me, in Jesus name.
14. Father Lord, let me not be put to shame before my enemies, in Jesus name.
15. Father Lord, exalt me by your power in, Jesus name.
16. Father Lord, redeem my soul by your power from the power of the grave, in Jesus name.
17. Father Lord, remind me daily that power belongs to you O' Lord, in Jesus name.
18. Father, you are the one who gives strength and power, so father give me power and might, in Jesus name.
19. Father, give me power to eat the fruits of my labor, in Jesus name.
20. Nothing is too hard for you O' Lord; my situation shall not be an exception, in Jesus name.
21. Father Lord, by your mighty power, open the ground and swallow my enemies, in Jesus name.
22. Let death spirit pass over me by your power, in Jesus name.
23. Father Lord, by your power, give me the anointing for multiplied blessing, in Jesus name.
24. Father, help me not to miss the presence of your power, in Jesus name.
25. By your power O' Lord, let me begin to experience the power of your kingdom, in Jesus name.
26. Let your power O' Lord reduce me, so you can have your way with me, in Jesus name.
27. Father, amaze the whole world by what you do with my life, in Jesus name.

28. Father Lord, help me by your power not to lose my sonship, in Jesus name.
29. Father Lord, let my power yield to your power daily, in Jesus name.
30. O' Lord let the power of Christ do miracle works manifest in me, in Jesus name.
31. Father, please turn my darkness to light, in Jesus name.
32. Let your power keep me delivered from the power of Satan, in Jesus name.
33. By your power, my father, help me to focus on invincible things, in Jesus name.
34. Let your power fill me with your hope, in Jesus name.
35. Let your power help me in my evangelism ministry, in Jesus name.
36. Father Lord, let your power give me the faith it takes to walk with you, in Jesus name.
37. Father let your power give me the wisdom it takes to live my life, in Jesus name.
38. Father, help me to begin to experience the power of your kingdom that is in power, in Jesus name.
39. The power of God that raised Jesus from the dead will not let anything die in me, in Jesus name.
40. Let the power in me remain greater than the power in the world, in Jesus name.

CHAPTER 25

FOUNDATIONAL POWERS

"If the foundations be destroyed what can the righteous do"? -Psalm 11:3.

1. Oh Lord, please repair any defect in my foundation, in Jesus name.
2. Father, help me fix whatever is in my foundation that would not carry my blessing, in Jesus name.
3. Father Lord, strengthen my foundation, so I can fulfill my destiny, in Jesus name.
4. Father Lord, help me repair the cracks in my foundation, in Jesus name.
5. Father Lord, please remove anything in my foundation that would cause my slow progress, in Jesus name.
6. Father give me powers to overcome satanic opposition in my foundation, in Jesus name.
7. Father let nothing in my foundation stop my purpose, in Jesus name.
8. Father, help me reverse any curse in my foundation against my finances, in Jesus name.
9. Let every altar against my foundation be destroyed, in Jesus name.
10. Let every sorrow and tragedy in my foundation be cast out, in Jesus name.
11. Let powers of disappointment in my foundation be consumed, in Jesus name.

12. Father Lord, frustrate the enemies attacking my foundation, in Jesus name.
13. Let the attackers of my foundation begin to fight against themselves, in Jesus name
14. Father Lord, help me overcome fear in my foundation, in Jesus name.
15. I bind and cast out lack of focus in my foundation, in Jesus name.
16. Father Lord, please keep your eyes in my foundation, in Jesus name.
17. Father Lord, let entities or groups waiting for the fall of my foundation be disappointed, in Jesus name.
18. Anger problem in my foundation be roasted, in Jesus name.
19. Foundational curses that would stop any of my breakthroughs be roasted, in Jesus name
20. Father Lord, set ablaze the satanic agenda in my foundation, in Jesus name.
21. Lord, remove my foundation from demonic associations, in Jesus name.
22. Let any evil name in my foundation receive a new name from God, in Jesus name.
23. Failure associated with my foundation be reversed, in Jesus name.
24. Let every access the enemies have into my foundation be blocked, in Jesus name.
25. Let every opening my foundation has to become closed to my enemies, in Jesus name.
26. Every program of failure in my foundation be nullified, in Jesus name.
27. Father, show your mercy on my foundation, in Jesus name.
28. Let any form of blindness in my foundation; receive sight now, in Jesus name.

29. Deafness in my foundation, receive hearing now, in Jesus name.
30. Let boldness come upon my foundation to do great things, in Jesus name.
31. Let the power to overcome every Goliath come upon my foundation, in Jesus name.
32. with the enemy in my foundation, break now, in Jesus name.
33. Let vows against my foundation be broken, in Jesus name.
34. Every arrow thrown at my foundation shall return to senders, in Jesus name.
35. O' Lord protect my foundation from demonic interference, in Jesus name

CHAPTER 26

INHERITED POWERS

Generational Curses

"For I, the Lord your God, am a jealous God, visiting the iniquity of the fathers upon the children to the third and fourth generations of those who hate me." -Exodus 20:5.

1. Heavenly father, please forgive me of all sins of my fore-fathers, in Jesus name.
2. Father Lord, help me break the anger you had toward my fore-fathers, in Jesus name.
3. Heavenly father, please remove me from ties to my father and fore-father's sins, in Jesus name.
4. Almighty father, separate me from every sin of my father's house and my mother's house, in Jesus name.
5. Father, Please nullify the effect of my fore-father's transgressions, in Jesus name.
6. My Lord, please do not hold me responsible for the sins of my mother's house, in Jesus name.
7. Heavenly father, please receive and keep me as a new creature in you, in Jesus name.
8. Heavenly father, do not let the sickness in my father's house affect me, in Jesus name.
9. My Lord, help me avoid the sickness that stopped my mother and her household, in Jesus name.
10. Every curse that stopped those before me shall not stop me, in Jesus name.

11. I shall cross the limits that were drawn for my father's house, in Jesus name.
12. Every ceiling that limited my mother's house shall not limit me, in Jesus name.
13. The sickness attributed to my father's house shall not affect me, in Jesus name.
14. The disease known to be a family problem in my mother's house shall not come near me, in Jesus name.
15. The curse that has had its way with my family tree will not affect me, in Jesus name.
16. As a new man, let no demons and gods served by my forefathers have dominion over me, in Jesus name.
17. Any gods that my fore-fathers promised to serve with his descendants all the days of their lives shall have no ties with me, in Jesus name.
18. I shall not inherit evil lands of my forefathers, in Jesus name.
19. I forsake all inherited demonic powers, in Jesus name.
20. I refuse to be a Prince or Princess for demonic powers, in Jesus name.
21. Let every evil altars that my father's house served all their lives be destroyed, in Jesus name.
22. Father Lord, destroy satanic altars my mother's house served, in Jesus name.
23. Father, change my name that was given to me relating to demonic powers, in Jesus name.
24. Father, deliver me from powers of my father's house that would limit me, in Jesus name.
25. Father let me not be numbered with those to be presented to demonic altars, in Jesus name.
26. Father, let no demonic land possessed by evil powers be shared for me, in Jesus name
27. I reject every word spoken by demonic priests into my family tree, in Jesus name.

28. I refuse to be possessed by demons that possess any member of my father's house, in Jesus name.

29. I refuse to be a part of the sacrifice my father's house agreed to make to evil gods, in Jesus name.

30. Father Lord, help me uproot every demonic statue that is made to be served by my mother's house, in Jesus name.

31. Father Lord, cancel every judgment over my father's house, in Jesus name.

32. Every obstacle standing on my way of progress with inherited rights to do so; Father Lord, help me wipe them out, in Jesus name.

33. I reject every challenge that led members of my father's house to go to demonic altars, in Jesus name.

34. Let me and any member of my father's house be stopped from being assigned one demon or another, in Jesus name.

35. Father, help me cleanse the land shared to me that was occupied by demonic powers, in Jesus name.

CHAPTER 27

IMAGINATIONS AND THOUGHTS

"Casting down imaginations and every high thing that exalts itself against the knowledge of God and bringing into captivity every thought to the obedience of Christ." -2Corinthians 10: 5:

1. Heavenly father, help me to have a new mind after your kingdom, in Jesus name.
2. Father Lord, please renew my mind to have pleasure in the affairs of your kingdom, in Jesus name.
3. Heavenly father, please help my mind to imagine greatness for me, in Jesus name.
4. Father Lord, help me to know that you are greater than my thoughts, in Jesus name.
5. Father Lord, help me to believe that my prayers are answered, in Jesus name.
6. Father Lord, help me to overcome negativity, in Jesus name.
7. Father Lord, let my thoughts tend toward prayer at all times, in Jesus name.
8. Father Lord, help me not to keep my mind on failure, in Jesus name.
9. Father, let my thoughts and imaginations be focused on you alone, in Jesus name.
10. Let my heart be on Godly Spiritual thoughts, in Jesus name.

11. Father, kill every thoughts and lustful imaginations, in Jesus name.
12. Heavenly father, help me accept that good things will happen to me, in Jesus name.
13. Almighty God, let my imaginations bring me good things, in Jesus name.
14. Heavenly father, help me to know to keep my mind and thoughts on your promises, in Jesus name.
15. Almighty father, help my thoughts not to destroy my faith, in Jesus name.
16. Let my mind be renewed and let thoughts acceptable to the Almighty fill my mind, in Jesus name.
17. Let my thoughts be subjected to the word of God, in Jesus name.
18. Let my thoughts be in my control always, in Jesus name
19. Let my thoughts and imaginations be in accordance with the word of God, in Jesus name.
20. Let my imaginations obey the will of God, in Jesus name.
21. Let my imaginations not lead me astray, in Jesus name.
22. Let my thoughts allow the anointing of God have its way with me, in Jesus name.
23. My thoughts give way for God's will to be established in my life, in Jesus name.
24. O Lord, my father, let my thoughts and imaginations help to increase my anointing, in Jesus name.
25. O' Lord, let my imaginations and thoughts be opened to communication with you, in Jesus name.
26. Father, deliver me from the battle in my thoughts and imaginations, in Jesus name.
27. Let my thoughts and imaginations be of love, in Jesus name.
28. Let my thoughts and imaginations lead me to my promotion, in Jesus name.

29. Father, help me overcome thoughts that would limit my prayers in Jesus name.
30. Let my thoughts and imaginations not limit me, in Jesus name.
31. Father, help me overcome self-condemnations, in Jesus name.
32. Let my thoughts be upgraded by the Holy Spirit, in Jesus name.
33. Let every of my challenges out of my thoughts become of no effect, in Jesus name.
34. Every attack against my thoughts must fail, in Jesus name.
35. Let the God in me shape my thoughts and imaginations, in Jesus name.

CHAPTER 28

LIMITATION FORCES

"And lest I should be exalted above measure by the abundance of the revelations, a thorn in the flesh was given to me, a messenger of Satan to buffet me, lest I be exalted above measure." -2 Corinthians 12:7.

1. Heavenly father expose every thorn the devil has placed to limit me, in Jesus name.
2. O' Lord, help me realize the limits the enemy has placed in my life, so I can pray to overcome them, in Jesus mighty name.
3. Father Lord, help me to realize the ceilings the enemy has placed over me as limitations, in Jesus name.
4. Almighty father, I shall overcome the limits set for my family, in Jesus name.
5. Father Lord, my faith shall exceed that of my father and mother, in Jesus name.
6. Holy Lord, help me to cross the limits that my family have never crossed before, in Jesus name.
7. The kind of money my father and my mother have never owned, let it be mine, in Jesus name.
8. Almighty father, give me powers to break down barriers set to hold me down, in Jesus name.
9. Father, give me the foresight to see beyond the limits drawn for me, in Jesus name.
10. Father Lord, establish my declarations and decrees, in Jesus name.

11. Let nothing pull me back from what the Lord has established for me, in Jesus name

12. Father Lord, strengthen my new foundation to hold my new grounds, in Jesus name.

13. O' Lord, prepare me to carry the responsibility that comes with a new blessing, in Jesus name.

14. Father, help me to overcome every temptation that would lure me into limitations, in Jesus name.

15. Father Lord, erase any written and unwritten law meant to limit me, in Jesus name.

16. Father, help me hear your voice, so I can stop from going where I am heading that would cause my limitations, in Jesus name.

17. Open my eyes Lord to see what would limit me, so I can avoid it, in Jesus name.

18. Open my ears Lord to hear what would limit me, so I can avoid it, in Jesus name.

19. Father, help me break associations that would cause my limitations, in Jesus mighty name.

20. O' Lord, surround me with people that would help me respond to marching forward, in Jesus name.

21. Father, help me silence voices from outside that would keep me where I am, in Jesus name.

22. Father Lord, help me quiet voices in me that would cause me not to move forward in, Jesus name.

23. Father, help me avoid the sin that would limit my progress, in Jesus name.

24. Father Lord, help me avoid a job or career that would cause a hindrance of my progress, in Jesus name.

25. Father, give me a spirit of obedience that would cause me not to be limited, in Jesus name.

26. Father Lord, remove me from bosses that would limit my progress, in Jesus name.

27. Father Lord, help me not to marry from a family that would cause my limitations, in Jesus name.
28. Father, help me overcome geographic limitations, in Jesus name.
29. Father Lord, help me not to live in a city where I would be limited, in Jesus name.
30. Help me O' Lord not to say things that would cause my limitations, in Jesus name.
31. Let me not experience, illness, sickness, or disease that would limit me, in Jesus name.
32. Let your living water flow into my vineyard to remove every limitation, in Jesus name.
33. Baptize me O' Lord to become unstoppable, in Jesus name.
34. Let no physical or spiritual barrier limit me, in Jesus name.
35. Father, help me enjoy your power that breaks barriers, in Jesus name.

CHAPTER 29

EVIL ALTARS

"But ye shall destroy their altars, break their images, and cut down their groves". –Exodus 34:13.

1. Father Lord, help me identify every evil altars in my life, in Jesus name.
2. Heavenly father, please expose the evil altars working against me, in Jesus name.
3. Almighty God help me destroy evil priest calling my name at evil altars, in Jesus name.
4. Heavenly father, for you see the evil altars erected for me, please let them fail, in Jesus name.
5. Almighty God every mirror by which enemies invoke my name, help me break them to pieces, in Jesus name.
6. Father, Lord, every evil altar that has my image, help me remove my images, in Jesus name.
7. Father, destroy every evil altar intended to stand against my blessings, in Jesus name.
8. Father, remove all evil altars that bring me failure in Jesus name.
9. Father, please separate me from evil altarserected before I was born, in Jesus name.
10. Evil altars in my community must bow to me, in Jesus name.
11. Evil altars asking for my blood be destroyed, in Jesus name.

12. Heavenly father, every altar that has risen against me must submit to the will of God for me, in Jesus name.
13. Every altar erected to take from me must be destroyed, in Jesus name.
14. Altars watching my steps is destroyed from my life, in Jesus name.
15. Altars erected to put me to shame, be destroyed, in Jesus name.
16. Every Altar laying wait for me, be destroyed in Jesus name.
17. Every evil altars holding unto the pillars of my life are destroyed, in Jesus name.
18. Every altar set up in blood in my father's house are destroyed today, in Jesus name.
19. Father Lord, remove the powers of small altars, in Jesus name.
20. Heavenly Father, I destroy every evil altar working against my destiny, in Jesus name
21. Every evil altar made to stop me, be destroyed today, in Jesus name.
22. Evil altar erected to stand at the point of my breakthrough, be destroyed, in Jesus name.
23. Altars set up to make me not to finish whatever I start, crumble now, in Jesus name.
24. Altars set up to make me invest in losing businesses, be destroyed, in Jesus name.
25. Altars set up to ring evil bell to drive away my customers be silenced, in Jesus mighty name.
26. Altars erected to nullify my favors, be destroyed, in Jesus name.
27. Altars erected to reduce the effectiveness of my prayers, be destroyed, in Jesus name.
28. Altars set up to lead me the wrong way, be destroyed in Jesus name.

29. Altars that bring me problems be destroyed, in Jesus name.
30. Altars of distractions from doing what am supposed to be doing, be destroyed, in Jesus name.
31. Altars that make me not to give God my best, be destroyed, in Jesus name.
32. Altars affecting my ministry, be destroyed, in Jesus name.
33. Altars that stand against my open doors, be destroyed, in Jesus name.
34. Altars that eat the fruits of the spirit from my life, be destroyed, in Jesus name.
35. Altars that stand against my faithfulness to God, be destroyed, in Jesus name.
36. Altars of lust erected against me be paralyzed, in Jesus name.
37. Altars erected to make me disobey God, be destroyed, in Jesus name.
38. My Lord destroy all altars that pull my spirit to where am not supposed to be in Jesus name.
39. Father Lord, remove perpetual altars that pull my family from the glory of God, in Jesus name.
40. Father, help me overcome basket altars, so I would see what I do with my money, in Jesus name.

CHAPTER 30

DIVINE ALTARS

"And he erected there an altar, and called it El Elohe Israel" -Genesis 33:20.

1. Let Divine altars of God speak for me daily, in Jesus name.
2. Let me meet with Divine altars everywhere I go, in Jesus name.
3. Let my prayer altars be anointed as Divine altar, in Jesus name.
4. Let our home be anointed as a Divine altar in Jesus name.
5. Let the powers in Divine altars speak against evil altars in my life in Jesus mighty name.
6. Let the glory of Divine altar rest on me in Jesus name.
7. Let the powers of Divine altar follow my wife and children wherever they go, in Jesus name.
8. Let me never serve God elsewhere, but only at Divine altars, in Jesus name
9. Let our church altar be linked with your Heaven's altar, in Jesus name.
10. Let heaven altar consume any other altar working against me, in Jesus name.
11. Let the blood of Jesus be the only blood speaking for me in, Jesus name.
12. Let the blood of Jesus destroy every other blood that has my name on it, in Jesus name

13. Father, let your presence be seen at any altar I worship you, in Jesus name.
14. Let your altar O' Lord watch over my activities, in Jesus name.
15. Let the altar of Jehova Nissi speak for me, in Jesus name.
16. Let the altar of Jehovah Jireh favor me daily, in Jesus name.
17. Father, let your altar be where I run into every day O' Lord, in Jesus name.
18. Father, let the power of your altar put a mark of Jesus on me, in Jesus name.
19. Father Lord, let me not play at your altar, in Jesus name.
20. Father Lord, let your altar answer when evil altar calls my name, in Jesus name.
21. Let the blood of Jesus continue to remember me and my household daily, in Jesus name.
22. Father Lord, let the Divine power of your heavenly altar extend into our business, in Jesus name.
23. Let your altar Lord, take away my daily sins, in Jesus name.
24. Father, let your Divine altar guide my children, in Jesus name.
25. Father, let your Divine altar be the protection my father and mother needs, in Jesus name.
26. Let the altar of Jehovah Sharma bring us the peace my family needs, in Jesus name.
27. Let the oil out of your altar be upon my head, in Jesus name.
28. Let the power of your altar swallow any of my anti progress altars, in Jesus name.
29. Father, let your Divine altar be a voice for me where I do not have a voice, in Jesus name.
30. Let your altar, O' Lord cancel every judgment rendered against me at evil altars, in Jesus name.

31. Father let your altar send fire against evil altars of my father's house, in Jesus name.
32. Divine altars let the goodness of God locate me, in Jesus name.
33. Divine altars of God, let my destiny remain intact, in Jesus name.
34. Every powers wrestling against my destiny, let Divine altars fight with them, in Jesus name.
35. Let Divine altars send Thunder, lightning, and the fire of God to destroy evil priests at evil altars, in Jesus name.

CHAPTER 31

POWERS AGAINST CHURCHES

"I say also unto thee, that thou are Peter and upon this rock I will build my church; and the gates of hell shall not prevail against it."- Matthew 16: 18.

1. Father, make my church one that the gates of hell cannot prevail against, in Jesus name.
2. Help us overcome every plan of Satan to pull down your church, in Jesus name.
3. Father Lord, let your fire operate in and outside of the church, so that Satan cannot have its way with the church, in Jesus name.
4. Father Lord, help forgive the sin of the leaders of the church, in Jesus name.
5. Heavenly father, give the leader a clear vision of the church, in Jesus name.
6. O' Lord, unify the members behind the vision of the Pastor of the church, in Jesus name.
7. Father Lord, help us remove every spirit of division, in Jesus name.
8. Almighty God, cause all your churches to unite as the body of Christ, in Jesus name.
9. Father Lord, every door the church has opened to the devil, please help us close the door, in Jesus name.
10. Father Lord, strengthen our church and all other churches with your fire, in Jesus name.

11. Every association the church has with evil elements, let the association break now, in Jesus name.
12. Father Lord, help us delete any event or activity that will not glorify your name in, Jesus name.
13. Help us expose any satanic influence in or around this church, in Jesus name.
14. We soak the grounds where the church is located in the blood of Jesus, in Jesus name.
15. Father Lord, we ask you to perfect the foundation of this church, in Jesus name.
16. Any weakness in the foundation of our church, help us remove it today, in Jesus name.
17. Father Lord, help every member to be faithful, in Jesus name.
18. Father, increase the faith of the members, in Jesus name.
19. Father Lord, help us with teachers that would teach your children the right way, in Jesus name.
20. Father Lord, let your truth prevail in our church, in Jesus name.
21. O' Lord, help us remove any reason by which your truth would be diluted in Jesus name.
22. Father Lord, give us your times for services in Jesus name.
23. Father, Lord, establish your evangelism ministry in our church, in Jesus name.
24. Father Lord, anoint your church to carry your fire, in Jesus name.
25. Father Lord, help us to link the Altar of our church with your altar in Heaven, in Jesus name.
26. Father Lord, let the members of our church understand tithes, so that we do not rob you in Jesus mighty name.
27. Father Lord, let our church take its place as the light of the world, in Jesus name.

28. Father Lord, we bring under our dominion everything that you created that has a name, in Jesus name.
29. Let your church remain unstoppable, in Jesus mighty name.
30. We take captive all powers that do not glorify Jesus in the area where my church is located in Jesus mighty name.
31. We uproot every buried powers that do not glorify Jesus where our church is located, in Jesus name.
32. We cleanse the building from powers that had dominion in the building before we took over, in Jesus name.
33. Help our church to fulfill its destiny and purpose, in Jesus name.
34. We pull down every strongman delegated by Satan to fight our church, in Jesus name.
35. Let the ground open and swallow every evil gathering against our church, in Jesus name.

CHAPTER 32

RESTORATION

"And I will restore to you the years that the locust hath eaten, the cankerworm, and the caterpillar, and the palmerworm, my great army which I sent among you"- Joel 2: 25.

1. Father, restore me to yourself, in Jesus name.
2. Father Lord, I pray that you restore me where I should have been while delaying to come to you, in Jesus name.
3. Almighty father, accept me as your son and remove me from where I kept myself, in Jesus name.
4. Father Lord, restore whatever I have lost, in Jesus mighty name.
5. Let my joy be restored to me, in Jesus name
6. The power that departed from me from evil association, be restored to me, in Jesus name.
7. Let the glory of God meant for me be restored to me, in Jesus name.
8. The anointing that God prepared for me let it return to me now, in Jesus mighty name.
9. Let the fruits of my labor that I did not get paid for be restored to me now, in Jesus name.
10. Let the years I wasted looking for what God wants me to do be restored, in Jesus name.
11. Let the times I spent serving others be paid now, in Jesus name.
12. Every money I lost through unprofitable investments be restored now, in Jesus name.

13. The time I spent listening to the wrong counselors be restored, in Jesus mighty name.
14. Father Lord, help me close every door I opened to the enemy that allows the enemy into my life, in Jesus name.
15. Restore my destiny, in Jesus name.
16. Father, draw me closer to you more than ever before, in Jesus name.
17. Let me repossess whatever was taken away from me, in Jesus name.
18. Every position I should have occupied, let me go back to it now, in Jesus name.
19. Every damaged foundation by my wrong association, let them be repaired, in Jesus name.
20. Father, take me to where you want me, in Jesus name.
21. Almighty father, break away chains of slavery and bondages from me and take me back as your son, in Jesus name.
22. Father Lord, restore in me any organ, blood, bones, marrow that I lost while I was away from you, in Jesus name.
23. Father Lord help me close every window I opened to let the enemy enter into my life, in Jesus mighty name.
24. Restore whatever was taken through my dreams, in Jesus name.
25. Whatever the enemies took from me while feeding me in the dreams, be restored to me, in Jesus name.
26. My destroyed prayer altars, be restored, in Jesus name.
27. Damaged relationship between my wife and I, be restored, in Jesus name.
28. Damaged relationship between my mother, my father and me, be restored, in Jesus name.
29. Damaged relationship with my child or children, be restored now, in Jesus name.

30. Every other relationship the enemies successfully damaged, be restored now, in Jesus name.
31. Every power that I let into my life, which now controls me, your time has expired, be gone now, in Jesus mighty name.
32. Satanic counsels I received, be reversed, in Jesus name.
33. Ungodly decisions I took, be changed now, in Jesus name.
34. The time I wasted outside of God, let me gain them back, in Jesus name.
35. Unprofitable work I did, let the earning return to me now, in Jesus name.

CHAPTER 33

SAFE TRAVELS

You must pray over all of your trips, whether they are short or long trips, so that the grace of God would protect and shield you and that you get the best of every travel.

"The stranger did not lodge in the street: but I opened my doors to the traveler" -Job 31: 32.

1. Father Lord, let all those I meet during my trip favor me, in Jesus name.
2. Father Lord, let my purpose for this trip be granted to me in your favor, in Jesus name.
3. Father Lord, be the driver of every car I would ride on during the trip, in Jesus name.
4. O' Lord, be the pilot of every plane I would fly in during my trip, in Jesus name.
5. Let my journey be one that comes with your mercy, in Jesus name.
6. Father, bless the water I will drink on my way and at my destination, in Jesus name.
7. Heavenly Father, bless the food I will eat according to your word during the trip, in Jesus name.
8. Father Lord, give me a spirit of discernment to separate the good people from the bad people that I would interact with during this trip, in Jesus name.
9. Father Lord, blot out delay from every step I take during this trip, in Jesus name.

10. Father guide my steps with your angels every step I take during this trip, in Jesus name.
11. Heavenly father, let me experience joy, happiness, and laughter during my trip, in Jesus name.
12. Father Lord, surround me with your shield of fire from territorial challengers, in Jesus name.
13. Father, let your heavenly warriors go in front and in my back and my sides as I go anywhere during this trip, in Jesus name.
14. I command my enemies to fall into the pit they may have dogged for me, in Jesus name.
15. Father Lord, help me to say the right thing at the right time to glorify you, in Jesus name.
16. Father Lord, let my actions support one who is your ambassador, in Jesus name.
17. Let people see you in me, so that someone would turn their lives to you by my trip, in Jesus name.
18. Father, protect me from evil intentions of those who want to use me, in Jesus name.
19. Almighty father, let no enemy see my weak side, in Jesus name.
20. Father, help me avoid the devil's avenue in Jesus name.
21. Father, let every knee that want to derail my trip bow now, in Jesus name.
22. Father, remind me that I am unstoppable with every step I take, in Jesus name.
23. Father Lord, please help me not to open windows for the evil ones, in Jesus name.
24. Heavenly Father, protect me from evil associations, in Jesus name.
25. Almighty Father, let none of my actions be ones that would initiate me into demonic community, in Jesus name.

26. O' Lord hide me in yourself everywhere I go, in Jesus name.
27. If any strong man is assigned against me, let the strong man die as soon as he is assigned, in Jesus name.
28. I surrender my will to you, so that your will would have its way with me on this trip, in Jesus name.
29. Let no one able to quench your light in me on my journey, in Jesus name.
30. Father Lord, set your helpers to locate me and help me on this trip, in Jesus name.
31. Father, let good testimonies of your love, favor, and kindness fill every step I take during this trip, in Jesus name.
32. No weapon formed against me shall prosper, in Jesus name.
33. I set ablaze every effort of the enemy designed to frustrate me on any turn, in Jesus name
34. I remove everything meant to cause me fear on this trip, in Jesus name
35. I will not die, I will not get hurt, I will not be involved in an accident, in Jesus name.
36. I nullify operation of evil forces in the area, in Jesus name.
37. I stop any evil powers that may want to travel with me, in Jesus name.
38. Father I scatter every evil re-arrangement of my trip, in Jesus name.
39. Father, expose every unfriendly friend that I may encounter, in Jesus name.
40. Father, open my eyes to get the best of the environment, in Jesus name.
41. Father, open my ears to hear what would change my life for the better, in Jesus name.

CHAPTER 34

COMPLETION

"Being confident of this very thing that he who has began a good work in you will complete it until the day of Jesus Christ" -Philippians 1:6.

1. Father, you are God that begin good things and finish them, so help me to finish whatever I start, in Jesus name.
2. Father, you are the beginning and the end, so help me to begin well and finish well, in Jesus name.
3. Heavenly father, I want to do only what pleases you, therefore, help me to start and end what I do, in Jesus name.
4. every distraction that would cause me to stop what I start, be removed from me, in Jesus name.
5. Every power set up against me to stop me must give way now, in Jesus name.
6. Every ceiling erected to make me stop at the point of my breakthrough must break into pieces, in Jesus name.
7. Wall of Jericho crumble now, in Jesus name.
8. Wherever I stop myself from completing what I started, Lord help me to give way to myself, in Jesus name.
9. Father, help me align my priorities to enable me complete what I have started, in Jesus name.
10. Lord, help me disassociate from acquaintances that would cause me not to be focused on what I have started, in Jesus name.

11. Let associates that would cause me to stop what I started become far from me, in Jesus name.

12. Let every voice that would cause me to stop what I started be silenced, in Jesus name.

13. Help me overcome physical challenges that would cause me to stop what I started, in Jesus name.

14. Father, let a name that would stop me after I begin a good thing be changed, in Jesus name.

15. Every filthy garment that would cause me to stop what I started, be burned up, in Jesus name.

16. Every power in my foundation that would stop me from completing what I started, be removed, in Jesus name.

17. Father, help me overcome personal experiences that would stop me from completing what I started, in Jesus name.

18. O' Lord let experiences of others that would stop me from a good thing I have started, in Jesus name.

19. Father Lord, help me encourage myself at the point of stopping what I started, so I can complete it, in Jesus name.

20. Father, let discouraging spirit be far from me, so I can finish what I stared, in Jesus name.

21. Father Lord, surround me with friends and families members that would encourage me to finish what I started, in Jesus name.

22. Father Lord, every territorial power that would stop me from completing what I have started receive the fire of God and be destroyed, in Jesus name.

23. Father, please forgive me of every sin that would stop me from completing what I started, in Jesus name.

24. Father Lord, help me not to take on another obligation that would stop me from what I started, in Jesus name.

25. Father, let your eyes guide me from the beginning to the end of whatever I start, in Jesus name.

26. Father Lord, give me the financial means to finish what I started, in Jesus name.

27. Father, give me the physical and emotional abilities to complete what I started, in Jesus name.

28. Heavenly Father, give me the patience to wait till I finish what I started, in Jesus name.

29. Father, help me with the knowledge and wisdom to complete whatever I start, in Jesus name.

30. Father, let me continue to see the end from the beginning, so I do not stop what I started, in Jesus name.

31. Father, help me not to destroy what I started with negative words of my mouth, in Jesus name.

32. O' Lord, help me speak life into what I started, so I do not stop, in Jesus name.

33. Father Lord, give me the faith to finish what I started, in Jesus name.

34. Father Let no evil manipulations derail me from what I started, in Jesus name.

35. Let no caged star stop me from finishing what I started, in Jesus name.

36. Let the blood of Jesus cover whatever I started, in Jesus name.

37. I refuse to be counted as a failure, in Jesus name.

38. Every limit that was set for my father's house or my mother's house not to complete what they started are erased, in Jesus name.

39. Father, destroy every war against me not to finish what I started, in Jesus name.

40. Father, let every gate that refuses me from finishing what I started be lifted now, in Jesus name.

CHAPTER 35

UNCOMMON AND UNUSUAL SUCCESS

"Then Isaac sowed in that land, and reaped in the same year a hundredfold; and the Lord blessed him" -Genesis 26:12.

1. Heavenly father, I want to sow good and reap great, in Jesus name.
2. Father, help me blot out powers that want to stop my abundant reaping, in Jesus name.
3. Father Lord, you are my shepherd, therefore I need your help for uncommon success, in Jesus names.
4. Father, bless me with uncommon favor and blessings, in Jesus name
5. Heavenly father, help me to succeed in all that I put my hands, in Jesus name.
6. Let me find the word that would lead to my uncommon breakthroughs, in Jesus name.
7. Daddy, let my hands be so blessed that whatever I touch would be successful, in Jesus name.
8. Father, let my success be good successes, in Jesus name.
9. Let my eyes be opened to see the area that would lead me to succeed, in Jesus name.
10. Father, let my ears be in tune with what I need to hear that would lead me to my success, in Jesus name.
11. Father, help me not to neglect the instructions that would lead me to unusual breakthroughs, in Jesus name.

12. Father, help me to be obedient to anyone you have sent my way that would lead me to success, in Jesus mighty name.

13. Let me be willing to obey and serve you, so that in return, you would bless me with unusual success, in Jesus name.

14. Let my blessings overtake me, in Jesus name.

15. Father, let my cup of blessing begin to run over, in Jesus name.

16. Despite all my adversaries let doors of unusual success be opened to me, in Jesus name.

17. Every gate that has shut me out of unusual success let those gates be lifted now, in Jesus name.

18. When I call for one person, let one thousand respond. I ask in Jesus name.

19. Let my successes be used to glorify your mighty name, in Jesus name.

20. Father, help me to triumph over all of my enemies, in Jesus name.

21. Let those who walk with me begin to experience triumphant life, in Jesus name.

22. Let the wicked receive their punishment, because they thought evil against me, in Jesus name.

23. Father, help me to do great exploits because I know you, in Jesus name.

24. Father, let your name be the pillar of my life always, in Jesus name.

25. Let the hand of God stretch toward my enemies and hold them down while I live my life, in Jesus name.

26. Father, help me enjoy the abundant life that Jesus Christ promised, in Jesus name.

27. Let the wealth of the sinners around me be transferred to me according to your word, in Jesus name.

28. Help me to live above only and never beneath, in Jesus name.
29. Let the power of your right hand strengthen and uphold me always, in Jesus name.
30. Father, let your generous Spirit lead me every day, in Jesus name.
31. Let the power of your might represent me in every battle, in Jesus name.
32. Father Lord, help me never to lack any good thing all the days of my life, in Jesus name.
33. O' Lord, let my progress be faster than any ordinary man, in Jesus name.
34. Father, make me an extra-ordinary man, in Jesus mighty name.
35. Let my wealth be used to take care of others in my community, in Jesus name.

CHAPTER 36

OPENED EYES AND EARS

"Open my eyes that I may see the wondrous things from your law" -Psalm 119: 18.

1. My Lord, my God open my eyes to see the opportunities you have put before me, in Jesus name.
2. Father Lord, open my eyes to see when to take steps, in Jesus name.
3. Father Lord, open my ears to hear when you say things that would benefit me in Jesus name.
4. Father Lord, help me see the hidden riches of this land, in Jesus name.
5. Father Lord, help me to hear of opportunities that would benefit me and my household, in Jesus name.
6. Father Lord, help me to see my helpers that would help me to my destiny, in Jesus name.
7. Heavenly father, help me see areas that would bring me down, so I can avoid them, in Jesus name.
8. Almighty God, help me see your messengers to me, in Jesus name.
9. Holy Father, help me to hear a voice I should follow, in Jesus name.
10. Holy Father, help me identify friends that I should avoid, in Jesus name.
11. Heavenly father, help me to hear your voice regarding the way I should go, in Jesus name.

12. Father Lord, help me to see and avoid evil associations in Jesus name.
13. Father Lord, help me to see and associate with godly associations to promote me, in Jesus name.
14. Father Lord, help me see and avoid opportunities that lead to nowhere, in Jesus name.
15. Father Lord, help me to hear from those I need to forgive to receive my breakthroughs, in Jesus name.
16. Father Lord, let the evil ones see your sign on me and avoid me, in Jesus name.
17. Heavenly father, help me to hear you when you call me, in Jesus name.
18. Almighty God, help me to see my hanging blessings, in Jesus name.
19. Holy God, let the whole world see your glory in my life, in Jesus name.
20. Heavenly father, let your kindness for me begin to show in my life, in Jesus name.
21. Father Lord, help me to see the day of your visitation, in Jesus name.
22. Almighty God, open my eyes to be able to discern good and evil, in Jesus name.
23. Father Lord, let me be a hearer and a doer of your word, in Jesus name.
24. Father Lord, help me to see where a need is that you would use me to meet, in Jesus name.
25. Father Lord, help me hear your daily instructions for my life, in Jesus name.
26. Father Lord, open my spiritual eyes, so I can see where I need to serve you, in Jesus name.
27. Father Lord, open my spiritual ears, so I can hear from you where I need to serve you, in Jesus name.
28. O' Lord, help me see in dreams the areas I need to work on, in Jesus name.

29. O' Lord, let me hear a word that would help move me to a higher level, in Jesus name.

30. Father Lord, reveal the deep and secret things to me, in Jesus name.

31. Heavenly Father, help me see and carry the light of life, in Jesus name.

32. Father Lord, please give me the vision of my life, in Jesus name.

33. Father Lord, please help me remove the veil from my eyes, so I can prosper, in Jesus name.

34. Father Lord, help me overcome vision killers, in Jesus name.

35. Father, help me to walk by faith and not by sight, in Jesus name.

36. Heavenly Father, help me to overcome dream killers, in Jesus name.

37. Father Lord, let my good dreams be established, in Jesus name.

38. Heavenly Father, help me cancel bad dreams that represent evil, in Jesus name.

39. Father Lord, give me the faith it takes to establish my visions, in Jesus name.

40. Father Lord, help me avoid associations that would derail my visions, in Jesus name.

41. Heavenly Father, help me to overcome every inherited spiritual blindness or deafness, in Jesus name.

CHAPTER 37

THANKSGIVING PRAYER POINTS

"In everything, give thanks for this is the will of God in Christ Jesus concerning you" -1 Thessalonians 5:18.

1. My father in heaven, I thank you for allowing me to see today, in Jesus name.
2. Today is a day you made for me, and I thank you Lord that I am not made for this day, in Jesus name.
3. Thank you Lord that you created the Sun and the moon to work for me, in Jesus name.
4. Thank you Lord that the powers of the stars shall work in my favor today, in Jesus name.
5. Thank you Lord for forgiving me of my sins, in Jesus name.
6. Thank you Lord for helping me forgive others who have wronged me, in Jesus name.
7. Thank you for separating me from others and that l am unique to you, in Jesus name.
8. Thank you Lord that you have not created anyone else like me, in Jesus name.
9. Thank you Lord for helping me break the ties I have with the evil ones, in the Mighty name of Jesus Christ.
10. Thank you Lord for helping me close every evil door I opened to evil workers, in Jesus name.
11. Thank you Lord for flushing out all foreign matters in my body, in Jesus name.

12. Thank you Lord for the Holy Spirit working to making me a better person for you, in Jesus name.
13. Thank you Lord for pulling down every stronghold in my life, in Jesus name.
14. Thank you Lord for destroying the yokes of the devil in my life, in Jesus mighty name.
15. Thank you Lord for setting me free from the power of darkness, in Jesus name.
16. Thank you Lord that you are a consuming fire, in Jesus name.
17. Thank you Lord that your word is quick and powerful, in Jesus name.
18. Thank you Lord that your word is like a fire and a hammer, in Jesus name.
19. Thank you Lord that you are not a man that would lie to me, in Jesus name.
20. Thank you Lord for giving me your word that carry your power, in Jesus name.
21. Thank you Lord for seen and unseen blessings, in Jesus name.
22. Heavenly Father, I thank you for all my known and unknown blessings, in Jesus name.
23. Father Lord, I thank you for giving me a name that is above every other name, in Jesus name.
24. Father Lord, thank you for hiding me under the shadows of the Almighty, in Jesus name.
25. I appreciate you for having me as your own child, in Jesus name.
26. Father Lord, I appreciate you for giving me your word that you keep, in Jesus name.
27. Thank you Lord, for when my heart condemns me, I have you to trust, in Jesus name.
28. Thank you for pulling me out of darkness into your everlasting light, in Jesus name.

29. Thank you Lord for your many provisions for me to have a better life, in Jesus name.

30. I appreciate it that I am a sheep in your flocks, in Jesus name.

31. Thank you for giving me a family that I love, in Jesus name.

32. I also appreciate it that you have given me a family that loves me, in Jesus name.

33. Thank you Lord that I have children and not Barren, in Jesus name.

34. Father, I thank you that I have a place I call my home and that I am not homeless, in Jesus name.

35. Thank you Lord for the gift of Salvation, to spend eternity with you when I die, in Jesus name.

36. Thank you Lord for your mercies, your grace, and your kindness, in Jesus name.

37. Thank you father that we can call you our father, in Jesus name.

38. Heavenly Father, I thank you Lord that I am alive and well and that I am not in the hospital, in Jesus name

39. Thank you Lord for opening my eyes to know you Lord, in Jesus name.

40. Thank you for sending Jesus to die for me to have a covenant with you, in Jesus name.

CHAPTER 38

CELESTIAL POWERS

"The sun shall not strike you by day nor the moon by night" –Psalm 121:6.

1. Every program against me in the sun, I neutralize it now, in Jesus name.
2. Every judgment against me in the heavens, I cancel them, in Jesus name.
3. Every power that hinders my prayers from ascending into heaven; let the consuming power of God burn down the powers, in Jesus name.
4. Father let my prayers become invincible to the enemies in the heavenly realm, in Jesus name.
5. O' Lord, let heavenly bodies rejoice when they hear my name, in Jesus name.
6. Father, erase every negative writing against me in the heavenly, in Jesus name.
7. Father Lord, kill every star fighting against my star and my destiny, in Jesus name.
8. Father Lord, help me clear every blur around my star, in Jesus name.
9. Father Lord, let my star refuse to cooperate with those trying to read it, in Jesus name.
10. Father Lord, let the power of the sun work for me, in Jesus name.

11. Heavenly father, let my life be like the rising and setting of the sun that nobody can stand on its path, in Jesus name.
12. Father Lord, let the power of the sun to smite be used to smite my enemies, in Jesus name.
13. Father Lord, let the favor of me surround the atmosphere, in Jesus name.
14. Father Lord, blind those spending time to watch my star, in Jesus name.
15. Father let those who have knowledge of the reading of my star begin to forget what the star says, in Jesus name.
16. Heavenly father, give negative reading to star gazers of my life, in Jesus name.
17. Father Lord, destroy the plans of those locating me through my star, in Jesus name.
18. Father Lord, let the moon become my friend, in Jesus name.
19. Father Lord, reverse every negative program of the enemy against me into the moon, in Jesus name.
20. From today I program into the moon my destiny according to the will of God, in Jesus name.
21. From today I program into the sun my destiny according to the will of God, in Jesus name.
22. From today, I program my destiny into the atmosphere according to the will of God, in Jesus name.
23. From today, my life shall attract favor from every of God's creations, in Jesus name.
24. I command a release of every of my blessings being held by the sun to come and locate me in Jesus name.
25. I command immediate release of my blessings being held by the moon to come and locate me now, in Jesus mighty name.
26. I command my blessings being held by heavenly powers to be released right now, in the name of Jesus

27. Those taking my name and image to the heavenly bodies, I command a disloyalty from the heavenly bodies, in Jesus name.

28. From today, I create a new friendship between me and the heavenly bodies, in Jesus name.

29. From today, every evil against me being carried into the heavenly bodies, let that evil splash over my enemies, in Jesus mighty name.

30. Those enemies walking around in the night, let the moon smite them for my sake, in Jesus name.

31. Every evil bird being sent to wrestle with me, let the atmosphere kill them, in Jesus name.

32. Father Lord, let your favor encompass me so much that the heavenly bodies know me as one that cannot be cursed, in Jesus name.

33. Father Lord, let me become a favored by the sun, in Jesus name.

34. Father Lord, let the moon favor me at night, in Jesus name.

35. Heavenly father, let other stars refuse to show which one is my own to my enemies, in Jesus name.

CHAPTER 39

DECREES AND DECLARATIONS

"You shall also decree a thing and it shall be established unto you the light shall shine on your ways" –Job 22: 28.

1. I shall serve God the rest of my life.
2. I put God above every other power.
3. I shall be great.
4. I am loved by everyone.
5. I am favored everywhere I go.
6. I am beautiful.
7. I get everything I want.
8. I am growing in the knowledge of God.
9. My eyes are opened to pursue my destiny.
10. I get what I want.
11. I live in the presence of God.
12. I live in the abundance of God's love.
13. I am a multi-millionaire.
14. I am the head.
15. I am above always.
16. I am a lender and I lend money to others.
17. I live in good health always.
18. I receive favor from everyone I meet.
19. I decree that illness, sickness, and diseases have no room and will never have room in my body.
20. All my enemies now love me.
21. I live in abundance of money all the days of my life.

22. Everything I look for shall find me.
23. I enjoy the favor of my Divine helpers.
24. The profit of this land is my own also and I am getting my share of the goodness of this land.
25. I am a winner and always a winner.
26. I walk in victory.
27. I am unstoppable.
28. I carry in my body the fire of the Holy Ghost.
29. Every dead thing around me has received the resurrection power of Jesus Christ.
30. I am covered in the blood of Jesus
31. My wife, my husband, my children, my business, my job are covered in the blood of Jesus.
32. My visions and prophecies are coming true.
33. I walk in the light of God.
34. I eat the fruits of all my labors.
35. The wealth of the sinners is transferred to me.
36. I shall rejoice throughout the day today.
37. Everything that happens to me today is happening for my benefit.
38. I am unstoppable.
39. Everyone loves me.
40. God's mercies and compassion are renewed in my life.
41. All my prayers are answered.
42. I shall perform miracles today with the name of Jesus.
43. My lost glory is restored to me.
44. My hanging blessings are released to me.
45. My helpers are locating me today.
46. The sun, the moon, and the stars are working to favor me today.
47. No evil shall come near me and my family members.
48. The goodness of heaven is opened to me.

49. One thousand Customers are calling me from the North, South, East and West to come and do business with them today.
50. God's kindness surrounds me and my family members.
51. I love everyone.
52. I forgive everyone who has ever hurt me and God has also forgiven me.
53. God's greatness is upon me.
54. I am doing great things with the name of Jesus.
55. Today men will favor me.
56. Women will favor me today.
57. My career is receiving the oil of God and it is getting better and better.
58. Death is far from me and my household members.
59. All my sorrows have turned into joy.
60. My needs are being supplied by God today.
61. The Lord has granted my promotion.
62. God has made me a lender.
63. All my judgments are canceled.
64. New business opportunities are opened to me.
65. I enjoy the protection of God with my family.
66. I shall not die, but live for God's glory.

CHAPTER 40

PRAYERS FOR LEADER

President and Governors

"But Moses' hands were heavy; ... and Aaron and Hur stayed up his hands, the one on the one side, and the other on the other side and his hands were steady until the going down" –Exodus 17:12.

1. Heavenly father, now that you have allowed these leaders to lead us, I pray that you give them the wisdom to lead this country, in Jesus name.
2. I also pray for the law makers that you give them a heart to make decisions that would turn peoples' hearts back to you, in Jesus name
3. Heavenly father, I lift up the decisions on the tables of the President and all of his decision team in your hands that you help them to make decisions that would favor the nation and my family, in Jesus name.
4. Father Lord, leading this country is not an easy task, because every decision favor some and hurts some, therefore I pray that your hands will be in the affairs of the President and his team now and always, in Jesus name.
5. Our father, your word says that the hearts of kings are in your hands, please tilt the heart of our leaders toward you Lord, in Jesus name
6. Father, let the President know that he needs you to lead these people and this nation, in Jesus name.

7. Heavenly father, touch the heart of our President, so he would know to lean and depend on you daily, in Jesus name.

8. Father Lord in his going out and coming in, let our President commit his ways to you O' Lord, in Jesus name.

9. Our father, order the steps of our President daily, so that you will delight in him and in our country, in Jesus name.

10. Almighty father, let the President enter into alliance with countries that will help exalt your name, in Jesus name.

11. Father Lord, use our President to bring unbelievers to you, in Jesus name.

12. Father Lord, let others see your glory in the life and ruling of our President, so that they will believe in you more and more, in Jesus mighty name.

13. Heavenly father, let this regime be a regime you will support, in Jesus name.

14. Heavenly father, let everyone see your hand in the affairs of our President, in Jesus name.

15. Almighty father, help me to continue to support the President daily in prayer throughout the regime of this President, in Jesus name.

16. Heavenly father, let this country be drawn to you during the regime of this President than ever before, in Jesus name.

17. Almighty God, please help me to do my part, in supporting this regime and helping through prayers to bring this country before you, in Jesus name.

18. Father Lord, please make this President the apple of your eyes daily, so when he calls on you, please answer, in Jesus name.

19. On the day of important decisions that affect all, please incline his heart to call on you O' Lord, in Jesus name.

20. Heavenly father, please open the eyes of the President to see the needs of these people, in Jesus name.

21. Almighty Father, open the ears of the President to hear from you regularly, in Jesus name.

22. Heavenly father, surround this President with team members that will help make decisions that will bring glory to your name, in Jesus name.

23. Heavenly father, through this President, let Heaven be opened to this country, in Jesus mighty name.

24. Almighty father, take your place as the Elohim, the head of the household of this country through this President, in Jesus name.

25. Father Lord, please protect and shield this President and his family from harm and danger all the days of his term, in Jesus name.

26. Heavenly father, use this President to bring peace to the world, in Jesus name.

27. Father Lord, please give this President the heart of Justice, in Jesus name.

28. Almighty God, Let this country experience your abundance through the leadership of this President, in Jesus name.

29. Father Lord, we break down powers that would influence this President to be a part of shedding innocent blood anywhere in the world, in Jesus name.

30. Father Lord, help this country to prosper spiritually everyday this President is in power, in Jesus name.

31. Father Lord, use this President as a point of contact to all other President all over the world, in Jesus name.

32. Father, touch the hearts of Christians to pray for their leaders daily, in Jesus name.

33. Let leaders dream dreams that would make them fear God, in Jesus name.

34. Heavenly Father, let our Christian leaders know the role of Christian leaders, in Jesus name.
35. Heavenly father, let the leaders not deny you when elected, in Jesus name.

CHAPTER 41

PRAYERS FOR NATIONS, STATES, AND CITIES

"Now therefore, I pray, if I have found grace in your sight, show me now your way that I may know you and that I may find grace in your sight. And consider that this nation is your people" –Exodus 33:13.

1. Father Lord, take back this country, in Jesus name.
2. Heavenly father, let my country's problems get your attention, in Jesus name.
3. Father Lord, the heart of our kings are, in your hands, turn them where you will, in Jesus name.
4. Heavenly father, let your will be done in this land, in Jesus name.
5. Father, let our laws that are made after your own laws not be twisted by man, in Jesus name.
6. Forgive all the states of all the wrongs doings contrary to your laws, in Jesus name.
7. Father Lord, have mercy on this nation, in Jesus name.
8. We have done more wrongs than Sodom and Gomorrah, please do not let your mercy run dry on us, in Jesus name
9. Help us to maintain our position in the world, in Jesus name.
10. Do not turn your anger on our country or take away your love from us, in Jesus name.

11. Father, raise up men and women that would honor you, in Jesus name.
12. Father, put in the hearts of your faithful and godly men to run and win elections, so that your name will not be destroyed by infidels who are running this country and states now, in Jesus name.
13. Father, please secure us from those who wants to destroy, us in Jesus name.
14. Father Lord, let the rich remember the poor in their daily lives, in Jesus name.
15. Father Lord, help us to reduce the rate of poverty in this land, in Jesus name.
16. Heavenly father let our country continue to be a big supporter of Israel, in Jesus name.
17. Father Lord, help us avoid committing sin that would turn your eyes away from us, in Jesus name
18. Father, I pray for peace to continue to reign in this land, in Jesus name.
19. Heavenly Father, let there continues to be unity to keep this country as one in Jesus name.
20. Let the people realize that sin is a reproach to any nation, in Jesus name.
21. Father Lord, send down your revival into this country, in Jesus name.
22. Father Lord, please raise your prophets and priest who will speak the truth and not only after money, in Jesus name.
23. Father Lord, create avenues for the voice of your prophets to be heard loud and clear in this country, in Jesus name.
24. Let prayers be returned to schools and public places in the states, cities, and this entire country, in Jesus name.
25. Father Lord, give our children teachers that have been appointed by you, in Jesus name.

26. Father Lord, please secure our boarders from foreign attackers, in Jesus name.
27. Father, we subdue rulers of darkness in the cities and states, in Jesus name.
28. Every idol that takes your place in this land, let your consuming fire burn them down, in Jesus name.
29. I declare this year a year of your presence, so let us enjoy your presence this year, in Jesus name.
30. Father Lord, we pray for rain that is ordered by you, in Jesus name.
31. Let your east wind take away the infirmity from us, in Jesus name.
32. Whatever the devil has ordered against this nation, I block and reject it today with the name of Jesus Christ.
33. Father, let repentance sweep across the nation in Jesus name.
34. Let those in power remember you in all of their decisions, in Jesus mighty name.
35. Father Lord, help us unite the churches, so we can all have one voice and in one accord before you, in Jesus name.

CHAPTER 42

DESTINY DESTROYERS

"I have seen servants on horses, while princes walk on the ground like servants". (This is a destroyed, altered, or changed destiny) -Ecclesiastes 10:7.

1. I will maintain the destiny that God created for me, in Jesus name.
2. Every cloud over my star is cleared now, in Jesus name.
3. I will flourish at my time that God ordered for me, in Jesus name.
4. My destiny shall be invincible to destiny killers, in Jesus name.
5. I refuse to surrender my destiny to destiny killers, in Jesus name.
6. Let blindness fall on those who secretly monitor my progress, in Jesus name.
7. Those who swallow destinies shall not swallow my own, in Jesus name.
8. I reject poverty from those who give poverty, in Jesus name.
9. The Lord will protect me, my wife, children, and siblings from those who engage in negative prayers against us, in Jesus name.
10. O' Lord protect me from those who change destinies while we sleep, in Jesus name.
11. Father Lord, protect me from associating with stagnating companions, in Jesus name.

12. Let unprofitable investments be distant from me, in Jesus name.

13. Father Lord, help me fight battles that would not let me reach my destiny, in Jesus name.

14. Help me overcome battles of the mind that would keep me from reaching my destiny, in Jesus name.

15. Every strongman delegated to keep me from fulfilling my purpose, let the strongman die now, in Jesus name.

16. I refuse to live under the status God made for me, in Jesus name.

17. Let every handwriting of failure against me be erased, in Jesus name.

18. Lord, open my eyes from spiritual blindness from seeing the path of my destiny, in Jesus name.

19. Lord, open my ears from spiritual deafness from hearing what would lead me to my destiny, in Jesus name.

20. Let every arrow fired into my destiny return to sender, in Jesus name.

21. Let those stopping my Divine helpers from helping me die, in Jesus name.

22. Father, lift me up from spiritual disabilities, in Jesus name.

23. O' Lord deliver me from fear that would keep me away from my destiny, in Jesus name.

24. Father Lord, deliver me from spiritual wife, in Jesus name.

25. Almighty God, deliver me from spiritual husbands, in Jesus name.

26. Father Lord, help me escape from financial prisons, in Jesus name.

27. Father let your jet carry me away from slow progress, in Jesus name.

28. Spirit of confusion, give way now, so I can move toward my promise land, in Jesus name.

29. Father, break every curse that would keep me from reaching my destiny, in Jesus name
30. Father, help me overcome geographic inhibitors, in Jesus name.
31. Foundational problems that would keep me from reaching my dreams and aspirations are repaired now, in Jesus name.
32. I uproot trees of failures against my destiny in Jesus name.
33. Father Lord, move me out of the way of my progress, in Jesus name.
34. Father Lord, forgive me of any sin that would stand on the way of reaching my dream, in Jesus name.
35. Those who exchange destinies will not locate my own, in Jesus name.
36. Father Lord, remove every evil man or woman sitting on my destiny, in Jesus name.
37. I de-program every program meant to walk me backward, in Jesus name.
38. Evil covenants meant to divert me toward the wrong destiny, be destroyed, in Jesus name.
39. O' Lord, expose unfriendly friends assigned to cunningly lead me away from my destiny, in Jesus name.
40. Father Lord, remove every filthy garment on me, in Jesus name.

CHAPTER 43

BREAKING CHAINS

"And, behold, the angel of the Lord stood by him, and a light shined in the prison: and he struck Peter on the side, and woke him up, saying get up quickly. And his chains fell off from his hands." –Acts 12:7.

1. Chains that tied me from reaching my abilities break now, in Jesus name.
2. O' Lord elevate me from where I am being held, in Jesus name.
3. Every chain tying me to my past is broken, in Jesus name.
4. Every chain I made myself that has held me down, be destroyed, in Jesus name.
5. Every chain made by others to keep me down, be broken, in Jesus name.
6. Father Lord, lift me out of every evil pits, in Jesus name.
7. Father Lord, lift me out of every evil holdings, in Jesus name.
8. Let the covenant of the Lord gather my virtues, blessings, and potentials and return them to me, in Jesus name.
9. Father Lord, purge pollutions from my life, in Jesus name.
10. Every wall that stands between me and my breakthroughs, let that wall fall down now, in Jesus name.
11. O' Lord, shine your light into my darkness, in Jesus name.

12. Let my spirit return to where I live, so I can enjoy my surrounding, in Jesus name.
13. Every block in my spiritual ears, be open now, in Jesus name.
14. Every caged star, be released now, in Jesus name.
15. Every promotion being held in captivity, escape and locate me now, in Jesus name.
16. I shall not be a dumping ground for my enemies, in Jesus name.
17. The battle that starts at the edge of my breakthrough, scatter now, in Jesus name.
18. Let me escape the fear that held me down in chains, in Jesus name.
19. Let those pursuing me away from my destiny, die, in Jesus name.
20. Let my Pharaoh drown in his Red Sea, in Jesus name.
21. Let those working to make me remain small, die, in Jesus name.
22. Every spiritual rivalry that has kept me from moving forward, die, in Jesus name.
23. Every marine power delegated to keep me from mainstream, die now, in Jesus name.
24. Father, help me avoid pits dug ahead of me, in Jesus name.
25. Let chains that have held my business break, in Jesus name.
26. Every demon holding onto my health release me now, in Jesus name.
27. Chains that are holding my womb, break, in Jesus name.
28. Chains the enemies have used to tie me to my father's house break now, in Jesus name.
29. Chains of failures, be broken, in Jesus name.
30. Chains of poverty, break from me now, in Jesus name.
31. Chains of affliction break from me now, in Jesus name.

32. Chains of disobedience to my God, be broken now, in Jesus name.

33. Chains dragging me to do the wrong thing from what God want, be destroyed now, in Jesus mighty name.

34. Bad dreams that have kept me in chains be destroyed, in Jesus name.

35. Let Herod and Pharaoh of my life die, in Jesus name.

36. My head reject crown of slavery, in Jesus name.

37. Every power sent to keep me low, give way now, in Jesus name.

38. My Lord, rebuke satanic powers holding down my prayers, in Jesus name.

39. Jesus! let your name go before me, be with me, and be behind me daily, in Jesus name.

40. I reject powers sent from evil altars to hold me from moving forward, in Jesus name.

CHAPTER 44

TREES OF LIFE

"Even so every good tree brings forth good fruit, but every bad tree bears evil fruit" Matthew 7: 17:.

1. Father Lord, locate and uproot all bad trees in my life, in Jesus name.
2. O' Lord every evil tree bearing bad fruits in my life be uprooted today, in Jesus name
3. Father Lord, whatever is watering bad trees in my life die, in Jesus name.
4. Every tree not bearing good fruits in my life, be uprooted, in Jesus name.
5. Let every tree that is not planted by God in my life, be uprooted, in Jesus name.
6. I am of God and any tree in my life must produce fruits to glorify God, in Jesus name.
7. Every useless tree meant to bring me down, be uprooted today, in Jesus name.
8. Father Lord, help me avoid eating out of the tree you have not allowed, in Jesus name.
9. Let the serpent not beautify evil tree for me, in Jesus name.
10. I shall avoid the wrong tree, in Jesus name.
11. Let me eat the fruit of life at the right time, in Jesus name.
12. Oh Lord my father, plant in my life the tree that produce milk and honey, in Jesus name.

13. Father Lord, prune every tree that would stand in my life, in Jesus name.
14. Let every tree in my life make me a pillar in your house, in Jesus name
15. Let all my enemies go and hang themselves on evil trees, in Jesus name.
16. Let the tree that keeps my spirit in Egypt dry up and die from today, in Jesus name.
17. Let every tree you have planted in my life be able to stand any and all weathers, in Jesus name.
18. Prove every tree in my life O' Lord, in Jesus name.
19. Help me separate trees for food and trees for seeding, in Jesus name.
20. Every good tree in my life shall yield their fruits in their season, in Jesus name.
21. When good trees of my life are yielding fruits, help me focus on you and not on the trees, in Jesus name.
22. Let the trees of my life remain watered always, in Jesus name.
23. Help me Lord, not to bring in foreign trees that would kill your trees in my life, in Jesus name.
24. Let your tree shade me and my family from evil, in Jesus name.
25. Let my neighbors not destroy the good trees of my life, in Jesus name.
26. Let my good trees spread across all coasts, in Jesus name.
27. Keep locusts away from consuming from my good trees, in Jesus name.
28. Let my children inherit the good of your good trees in, in Jesus name.
29. Let nothing dislodge me from my good trees, in Jesus name.
30. Let kings and princes of the land know of my trees, in Jesus name.

31. Let my good trees be a blessing to all those who know me, in Jesus name.
32. Let me receive knowledge from your good trees in my life, in Jesus name.
33. Let good trees stand in the lives of my wife, my children, my siblings, in Jesus name.
34. Let our good trees flourish while the bad ones die, in Jesus name.
35. Let every tree that stands in my life be one you have approved, in Jesus name.
36. Qualify me to eat the fruit of life, in Jesus name.

CHAPTER 45

COVENANT

"As for you also, because of the blood of your covenant, I will set your prisoners free from the waterless pit." --Zechariah 9:11.

"...This is the Blood of the covenant, which God has commanded you" –Hebrews 9:20.

"And he said to them, this is my blood of the new covenant, which was shed for many" -Mark 14:24.

1. Father Lord, I thank you for the new covenant in the blood of Jesus, in Jesus name.
2. O Lord, let the covenant speak for me where I have a voice or where I have no voice, in Jesus name.
3. My father, my father, let me enjoy the covenant all the days of my life, in Jesus name.
4. Father, help me stay in my place where the covenant would always cover me, in Jesus name.
5. Father, let the mercies of the covenant blot away all of my sins, in Jesus name.
6. Oh Lord my father, let my life be renewed by the covenant I have through the Blood of Jesus, in Jesus name.
7. Father, let the covenant break down every access that I was blocked from, in Jesus name.
8. Father Lord, let the new covenant destroy every other old covenants that I am currently under, in Jesus name.

9. Father, let the covenant tear down every stronghold that is currently over my life, in Jesus name.

10. Almighty God, let the covenant open doors into unusual breakthroughs for me, in Jesus name.

11. Father, help me enjoy all that the covenant has to give to man and to the glory of God in Jesus name.

12. Father, help me to be plugged into all that the covenant has to give, in Jesus name.

13. Father Lord, let the mark of the covenant be pronounced in my life that any other covenant would know I belong to another covenant, in Jesus name.

14. Heavenly father, let my name be written in the book of life, because of the covenant, in Jesus name.

15. Father, let your covenant draw me closer to you, O' Lord, in Jesus name.

16. Father, let the covenant I have through Jesus guide me always, so I can remain in your will always, in Jesus name.

17. Father, let the covenant show up wherever my name is being mentioned for evil, in Jesus name.

18. Holy Lord, let the covenant absorb me from the judgment of man, in Jesus name.

19. Father, do not let me go to where the covenant would not cover me, in Jesus name.

20. Father, help me enjoy the glory that the covenant brings, in Jesus name.

21. My father, my father, cover me and my household with the blood of the covenant, in Jesus name.

22. Father Lord, let the covenant turn my weaknesses to strength, in Jesus name.

23. Father, every soul ties and covenants I have with others, let the power of this covenant break me out of those, in Jesus name.

24. Heavenly father, let the covenant I have through the blood of Jesus cover my household, in Jesus name.
25. Almighty God, let the covenant shield me and my family from the evil happening to others, in Jesus name.

CHAPTER 46

REPENTANCE PRAYER AFTER DISOBEDIENCE

"For godly sorrow works repentance to salvation not to be repented of: but the sorrow of the world works death" -2 Corinthians 7:10.

When you realize that you were called, but you did not answer, you need this prayer of genuine repentance.

1. "Mercy upon me, O God, according to your loving kindness; according to the multitude of your tender mercies, blot out my transgressions" - Psalm 51:1.
2. Father Lord, I thank you for revealing my disobedience to me, in Jesus name.
3. I seek your mercy O' Lord; grant me abundance of your mercy, in Jesus name.
4. Every influence of disobedience, receive the fire of God now, in Jesus name.
5. I need your power to get up when you call me, so Lord, grant me the power, in Jesus name.
6. My flesh is always weak, so Lord, I need your strong hand that would pull me to obedience daily, in Jesus name.
7. Retool my spiritual ears to hear clearly from you, in Jesus name.
8. Anything in me that would not submit to your will, O' father, please take it out, in Jesus name.

9. Every tree of disobedience in me that would cause me to disobey you, father Lord, uproot it now, in Jesus name.

10. Father Lord, silence any counter voice that would lead me astray, in Jesus name.

11. Father, deliver me from the punishment of disobedience, in Jesus name.

12. You are the porter and I am the clay, make and remold me to one who will hear and obey you always, in Jesus name.

13. Father, I have nowhere to run to, but run back to you, accept me back, in Jesus name.

14. Father, help me overcome whatever has makes me disobey you O' Lord, in Jesus name.

15. Disassociate me from groups or individuals that would cause me to disobey you in the future, in Jesus mighty name.

16. O' Lord, help me tune down my will and turn up your will for me, in Jesus name.

17. Father Lord, open my ears and my eyes to hear and see your instructions clearly, in Jesus name.

18. Father, help me remove obstacles that may have made me to disobey you, in Jesus name.

19. Father, help me walk away from excuses that have caused me to disobey you, in Jesus name.

20. Father Lord, help me trust you more, so every doubt would be eliminated in future, in Jesus name.

21. Father, am ready for your use, therefore prepare me for your use, in Jesus name.

22. The purpose for your sending me, please do not delete it, in Jesus name.

23. If my excuse was that I forgot the instructions, father, give me a heart of remembrance, so I would not forget your instruction in the future, in Jesus name.

24. Father, restore our relationship, in Jesus name.

25. Father, please give me the faith it takes to walk with you, in Jesus name.
26. Father, remove my unbelief and increase my faith, in Jesus name.
27. Heavenly father, help me not to associate with anyone or group that would reduce my faith, in Jesus mighty name.
28. Father, help me associate with those who will help me maintain or increase my faith, in Jesus name.
29. Father, grow my faith, in Jesus name.
30. Let your name be glorified by the fruits of my life, in Jesus name.
31. Confirm every future message with your signs, in Jesus name.
32. Father, let any contrary sign the devil would show me to deceive me catch fire, in Jesus name.
33. Father, remove fear that would cause me to disobey you, in Jesus name.
34. Let me not be condemned by my disobedience, in Jesus name.
35. Do not take that ministry or message away from me and give it to another by my disobedience, in Jesus mighty name.
36. Do not chase me out of your kingdom by my disobedience, in Jesus name.
37. Let my past labor toward your name in the past be retained in my account, in Jesus name.
38. Father, I come back home like the prodigal son did and please accept me back, in Jesus name.
39. Father Lord, do not give me a way of escape from your presence next time in, Jesus name.
40. Grant me your grace to carry out your assignment, in Jesus name.
41. Help me to know that you will not send me where your grace would not go with me, in Jesus name.

CHAPTER 47

TONGUES OF GOD

"Then the Angel of God spoke to me in a dream, saying, 'Jacob' And I said, Here I am." -Genesis 31:11.

General Break through Prayers Pray each of these prayers for 2 minutes

1. Oh Lord, I will not let you go except you bless me, in Jesus name –Genesis 32:26.
2. Oh Lord, show me your glory, in Jesus name - Exodus 33:18.
3. "O' Lord, give to your servant an understanding heart to discern between good and evil, in the name of Jesus -1 Kings 3:9.
4. O' Lord, enlarge my coast, in Jesus mighty name– (A prayer of multiplication, Spread, grow, and extend beyond borders) -1 Chronicles 4:10.
5. O' Lord arise and let my enemies be scattered, in the name of Jesus –Psalm 68:1.
6. O' Lord God answer me by fire, in Jesus mighty name, --1 Kings 18:24.
7. Where is the Lord God of Elijah (Prayer to gain access – when there is a road block, there is a standstill, no progress) Open this opportunity to me, in Jesus name. - 2 Kings 2:14:
8. O' Son of David have mercy on me, in the name of Jesus -Mark 10:47.

9. O' Lord, behold their threatening, in Jesus name -Acts 4:29.

10. O' Lord make me a mysterious wonder, in Jesus name (Just like wind – I want to be as mysterious as the wind – nobody knows my going or coming) -John 3:8

These are follow-up prayers:

11. Chaos, enter the camp of my enemies, in the name of Jesus.

12. Eyes of darkness against me to monitor me – Be blinded, in Jesus name.

13. Any power taking my name to the coven – die with your coven, in Jesus name.

14. O' Lord arise and overthrow the wicked powers in my life, in Jesus name.

15. Altars of darkness made to work against my progress – catch fire, in the mighty name of Jesus.

16. Every power challenging my moving forward – die, in the name of Jesus name.

17. Satanic wind blowing against my forward movement – be terminated now, in Jesus mighty name.

18. God of favor – appear in my life quickly, in the name of Jesus.

19. Every charm working against my life – Receive the fire of God, in the name of Jesus.

20. Doors opened to admit my children into witchcraft powers, be closed against my children, in Jesus name.

21. Every programmed serpent against me, Blood of Jesus flush out the serpent, in Jesus name.

22. Darkness over my life, receive the light of God now, in Jesus name.

23. O' Lord God of Elijah, advertise your power in my life, in Jesus name.

24. Strongman of financial embarrassment die from my finances, in Jesus name.

25. Strong woman of financial embarrassment – die from my money, in Jesus name.

26. Every power assigned to put me to shame – be destroyed, in Jesus name.

27. My head, my head, I call you forth to be lifted up by fire, in Jesus name.

28. Every wicked grip upon my life – lose your hold, in Jesus name.

29. Holy Ghost fire – destroy garments of reproach in my life, in Jesus name.

30. My stubborn enemy – receive arrow of shame, in Jesus name.

31. O' God arise and bring miracles into my life, in Jesus mighty name.

32. Any grave power holding my testimony, release my testimony and scatter, in Jesus name.

33. Every opposition to my laughter – clear away now, in Jesus name.

34. Program of failure programmed against me – be destroyed now, in Jesus name.

35. Evil birds swallowing my virtues – be arrested and be destroyed now, in Jesus name.

36. Arrow of poverty, go back to your sender, in Jesus name.

37. Strange dreams bringing strange problems into my life – scatter, in Jesus name.

38. Witchcraft powers against my life – be destroyed, in Jesus name.

39. Evil wind blowing against my rising be still now by the counter wind of God, in Jesus name.

40. Every demonic arrangement meant to pull me down – scatter, in Jesus name.

CHAPTER 48

KILL OR GIVE LIFE

Use Your Tongue to bring death or bring life. You can also use your tongue to send death or send life to others.

"Death and life are in the power of the tongue and they that love it shall eat the fruit of it" - Proverbs 18:21.

1. Every power against my rising, I command you to die quickly, in Jesus name.
2. Every demon assigned against my rising – Die today, in Jesus name.
3. Every witch or wizard pointing evil fingers against me – I kill you with my tongue, in Jesus name.
4. Every power calling what I do to go under – I kill the power today, in Jesus name.
5. Every agenda to terminate my progress – I kill you with my tongue, in Jesus name.
6. I kill with my tongue every power that terminated those before me and ready to terminate my own, in Jesus name.
7. I kill every spirit that wants to use serpentine tricks to stop me, in Jesus name.
8. I kill every serpentine spirit following me to destroy my own, in Jesus name.
9. I kill every power of the night that press negative issues into me at night, in Jesus name.

10. I kill every power of the night that comes into my dwelling without my permission, in Jesus name.
11. I close my doors and windows against every power of the night, in Jesus name.
12. The enemy that comes to me at night – I kill you with my tongue, in Jesus name.
13. I turn disgrace against you; every disgrace that the enemy has prepared for me, in Jesus name.
14. I call the fire of God to come down and consume every satanic and demonic deposits in my life, in Jesus name.
15. I nullify powers behind every point of contact the enemy may have left with me, in Jesus name (Understand this prayer point - Enemy will leave something with you, so that they can in turn reach you as long as that thing is with you).
16. Anyone who has volunteered to stop my marching forward – I kill you with my tongue, in Jesus name.
17. I expose and I curse evil man or woman pretending to be a friend, in Jesus name.
18. Every agenda with my name on it that is against my will – I kill you, in Jesus name.
19. Every agenda being held by agent of darkness against me – I kill you, in Jesus name.
20. Every agenda planting evil in my life – I kill you, in Jesus name.
21. Any program in the air to restrict me – I kill you with my tongue, in Jesus name.
22. Every territorial power that is standing against my activities – I kill you with my tongue, in Jesus name.
23. Every territorial power ruling in my business world I dethrone and kill you by my tongue in Jesus name.
24. Every territorial power restricting my business life – I kill you today with my tongue, in Jesus name.

25. Every territorial gate standing against what I do, give way now or die, in Jesus name.
26. Every territorial gate standing to make me fail, I kill you today, in Jesus name.
27. Everything the enemy has killed in my life – receive new life now, in Jesus name.
28. I kill frustration spirit following me around, in Jesus name.
29. I receive the favor of God to upset frustration spirit, in Jesus name.
30. I call new life into organs of my head now, in Jesus name.
31. I call new life into my exterior organs, in Jesus name.
32. I call new life into my internal organs in, Jesus name.
33. I kill and destroy satanic powers living in my house without my permission, in Jesus name
34. I subdue powers manipulating my affairs without my permission, in Jesus name.
35. Every power ruling over my life through legal grounds I kill you with my tongue, in Jesus name.
36. Every power ruling over my life through illegal grounds I kill you with my tongue, in Jesus name.
37. Any grounds the enemies are standing on to attack me, let the grounds open and swallow them, in Jesus name.
38. Any ground I lost through demonic manipulations – I recover the grounds today, in Jesus name.
39. I take my place where I am supposed to be, in Jesus name.
40. Anyone sitting on my seat – I dethrone you today, in Jesus name.
41. I give new life into my school, in Jesus name.
42. I give new life to my business, in the name of Jesus.
43. I give new life to my career, in Jesus name.
44. I give new life to my relationships, in Jesus name.

45. I give new life to my ministry, in Jesus name.
46. I give new life to my destiny, in Jesus name.
47. Any of my falling star, go back to the sky and begin to shine brighter, in Jesus name.
48. Every blurred star, begin to shine again, in Jesus name.
49. I give new life to my fortune, in Jesus name.
50. Every buried virtue, receive new life now, in Jesus name.

CHAPTER 49

SPEAKING IN UNKNOWN TONGUES

"For he who speaks in tongue does not speak to men but to God...." -1 Corinthians 14:2.

"Likewise the Spirit also helps our infirmities: for we know not what we should pray for as we ought: but the Spirit itself makes intercession for us with groaning which cannot be uttered." – Romans 8:26

Pray in tongue as part of your daily pray life and the Lord would use them to address your issues.

Praying in tongues in speaking to your situation without know what you are praying about. By speaking in tongues, you are addressing angels, and talking to God about what you need done for you.

Speaking in tongues as prayer and speaking to God is different from speaking in tongues as in prophesying. Use speaking in tongues to address areas you need to address, but that you are not aware of. Which means on a daily basis, after or before praying with understanding, you need to include praying in tongues as a part of praying for areas you do not know you need to pray about.

a. Father, give me the power to speak in tongues, in the mighty name of Jesus.

b. Heavenly father, help me to know the power in praying in tongues, in Jesus name.

c. Almighty God, do not let me overlook the power of praying in tongues, in Jesus name.

CHAPTER 50

PRAISE

Nothing replaces praise and worship to God. Spending time after midnight to praise God even for 15 minutes brings breakthroughs.

Read this Bible verses several times until you are at peace that you have received your breakthrough and deliverance.

"But at midnight Paul and Silas were praying and singing hymns to God, and the prisoners were listening to them. Suddenly there was a great earthquake, so that the foundations of the prison were shaken; and immediately all the doors were loosed." - Acts 16:25-26.

"Enter into His gates with thanksgiving, and into His courts with praise. Be thankful to Him, and bless His name"
– Psalm 100:4:

Psalm 150

"Praise the Lord!"
Praise God in His sanctuary;
Praise Him in His mighty firmament!
Praise Him for His mighty acts; Praise Him according to His excellent greatness! Praise Him with the sound of the trumpet; Praise him with the lute and harp! Praise Him with the timbrel and dance; Praise Him with stringed instruments and flutes!

Praise Him with loud cymbals; praise Him with clashing cymbals! Let everything that has breath praise the Lord. Praise the Lord!

Prayers of Praise and Worship:

1. Father in the name of Jesus, I praise and worship you now, in the name of Jesus.
2. Father Lord, you alone are worthy of my praise and worship, in Jesus name.
3. Almighty God, you alone deserve my adoration and gratitude, in Jesus name.
4. Almighty God, my heart, my soul, and my flesh surrender to you in praise of your name alone, in Jesus name.
5. My father, my father, I bow my soul to you in praise of your name, in Jesus name.
6. Heavenly father, receive my praise and worship, in Jesus name.
7. Father Lord, let my heart praise you day and night, in Jesus name.
8. Father Lord, I praise and thank you that I am alive and well, in Jesus name.
9. Heavenly Lord, let my altar of praise stand strong, in Jesus name.
10. My father, my father, let the power of praise of my lips be from my heart, in Jesus name.
11. Father Lord, let my praise bring down powers battling with me, in Jesus name.
12. Let my praise Oh Lord, destroy powers reigning in my geographical locations, in Jesus name.
13. Heavenly father, let my praise destroy power of darkness operating in my neighborhood, in Jesus name.

14. Father Lord, let my praise dethrone powers of darkness that control my state and my country, in Jesus name.

15. Almighty God, let the spirit of praise raise up the dead that are of God in my neighborhood and my state, in Jesus name.

16. Father Lord, let the praise of your people take control of powers of darkness operating against the government of this country, in Jesus name.

17. Heavenly father, hear and respond to the praise of your people, in Jesus name.

18. Oh Lord my father, let my praise be acceptable to you today and every day, in Jesus name.

19. Father Lord, help me make more time in the praise of your name, in Jesus name.

20. My father, my father, let my praise bring honor to your name, in the might name of Jesus Christ.

21. Father, let my life be a praise and worship to you, in Jesus name.

22. Heavenly father, I praise and worship you, because I still have my eyes to see, in Jesus name.

23. Heavenly father, I thank you that my tongue and teeth are still in place, in Jesus name.

24. My father, my father, I thank you that all of my internal organs are intact, in Jesus name.

25. Father Lord, whether I receive answers to my prayers or not, you remain the Most High forever, in Jesus name.

26. Thank you Lord that you are not afraid of any man, and you are not answerable to any man, in Jesus name.

27. Thank you Lord that you are God that keeps your word to man, in Jesus name.

28. Father, I rejoice that I have confidence in you in all things, in Jesus name.

29. Heavenly Father, I praise your name for giving us the name, Jesus, which is a name above all other names, in Jesus name.
30. Father Lord, I thank you for being the author and finisher of my faith, in Jesus name.
31. Heavenly father, I thank you for granting us your resurrection power, in Jesus name.
32. Almighty God, I praise and worship you that every dead things in my life are coming back alive are coming back alive, in Jesus name.
33. Heavenly father, I thank you that I have food on my table every day, in Jesus name.
34. Almighty God, I appreciate you that I still have a family member.
35. Almighty God, I honor your name for your good over all nations, in Jesus name.
36. Heavenly father, I thank you for all the people you have put in my life, in Jesus name.
37. My father, I thank you for my journey of life so far and I am grateful that you have arranged them for my good, in Jesus name.
38. Almighty God, I thank you for all of your promises in the Bible, in Jesus name.
39. Father Lord, I praise your name that you have located me where I live and where I work, in Jesus name.
40. Heavenly father, I worship you that you call me your ambassador, your vessel, your branch, and your child, in Jesus name.

CHAPTER 51

WHAT CHRISTIANS MUST KNOW!

Life are spiritual:

It means that powers that control the world is spiritual powers and what you see is a manifestation of what happened in the spiritual realm.

a. If you fight with anyone, the fight was orchestrated from the spirit realm.
b. If you have a breakthrough, it was achieved in the spirit realm.
c. If a marriage is working or not working, it is a result of what happened in the spiritual realm.
d. The Bible describes the spirit realm this way: 2 Corinthians 4:18: "While we look not at the things which are seen, but at the things which are not seen, for the things which are seen are temporary, but the things which are not seen are eternal".
e. This Bible verse has a deep implication on where your focus should be. Any problem you have arose out of a spiritual realm and the permanent solution is in the spiritual realm. Any physical solution is temporary.
f. "Put on the whole armor of God that you may be able to stand the wiles of the devil. For we wrestle not against flesh and blood, but against principalities,

powers, against the rulers of darkness of this world, against spiritual wickedness in high places" – Ephesians 6:11-12.

g. Fights that look minor at home, at work, with strangers, in the park, at the beach, in traffic, and so forth are initiated in the spiritual realm, so avoid fighting, but address conflicts with prayers and do not fall for enemies' tricks.

CHAPTER 52

CONCLUSION

"Finally brethren, be strong in the Lord and in the power of His might" - Ephesians 6:10

"Those who value their lives are those who recognize that God is a Spirit. God made everything we see today from the spiritual realm and that spiritual realm controls all things we see. If you want to take control of the spiritual side of your life, you need to get strong prayer points this book contains them. It means you are taking control of where your life heads."

Whatever you want to bring to your reality or to manifestation, can only happen by engaging the spirit realm. Get this prayer handbook as a step toward your destiny. Get one for each of your loved ones.

If you do not fulfill your purpose just because you could not pray is a lazy way to have lived. Do not live without fulfilling your purpose; stop the enemy who wants to stop you. The enemy seriously wants to stop you from achieving your dream and your purpose, your aspirations, and to stop you from entering your promised land, your destiny.

The enemy wants you to disappoint your maker and that is why you must learn how to pray to get result, which is the only weapon you have to fight back. When things are going well, we tend to relax, but the enemy is always planning strategies to bring us down.

Use this high powered prayer book to fight back for you and your family. Achieve your optima by employing the power to fight back. Use it every day, because the enemy does not go on vacation!

CHAPTER 53

HEAVEN'S COURT

But the judgment shall sit, and they shall take away his dominion, to consume and destroy it unto the end - Daniel 7:26:

And the kingdom and dominion, and the greatness of the kingdom under the whole heaven, shall be given to the people of the saints of the Most High, whose kingdom is an everlasting kingdom, and all dominions shall serve and obey him. (Whatever was dominating you is what you shall dominate after the judgment from the courts of heaven) Daniel 7: 27:

When your prayers seems like they are not receiving God's attention – Your case may be held up in Heaven's court.

Let us come boldly to the throne of Grace and obtain mercy and find grace to help in the day of need. - Hebrews 4:16:

No special skill, knowledge, profession are needed or required to appear before our father in heaven's court, but:

    a. You must be born again.
    b. You must know how to imagine yourself in a courtroom with a judge and others.
    c. Be honest with yourself – God and everyone present know you better than you know yourself.
    d. You are not there to defend yourself.

e. The judgment in your favor is out of mercy, because you confessed that you are wrong.

f. The judge is your father and your friend.

1. **How is in the court setting?**
   a. Seats like any other courtroom.
   b. A court setting.
   c. Your accusations.
   d. Some of the accusations may be from your bloodline – dating back 20 generations.

2. **Who is in Heaven's Court?**
   a. Our Father – the Righteous Judge – the Most High God.
   b. Bailiffs: the Angels of God; that always surround our Father.
   c. Angels – Surrounding the courtroom.
   d. Saints that have passed on and those who are part of the Counsel of God – As witnesses.
   e. The Holy Spirit, Teacher, Comforter, Helper, and the 7 Spirits of God.
   f. Jesus Christ – Our advocate and our Priest.
   g. The Blood of Jesus is there to speak for you.
   h. The 24 Elders (This is a position and can be occupied by anyone).

3. **What kinds of Accusations are present: Daniel 7:10 (Books opened)**
   a. Killing, stealing, destroying; such as abortions.
   b. Lies and exaggerations.
   c. Back stabbing, back biting, and false tales.
   d. Disobedience to God's instructions.
   e. Disobedience to God's Ten Commandments.
   f. Record of no commitment to God's work.
   g. Unfaithfulness and every unfaithful ways.

h. Doing things God does not want you to do.

i. Not doing what God wants you to do.

j. Record of fornication and or adultery.

k. Not occupying your place.

l. Sins of Bloodline.

m. Unholy Dedications.

n. Eating at unholy/idolatry places

o. Swearing and swearing falsely

p. Unpaid vows.

q. Pornography – your own and those of your bloodline.

r. Covenants in entered by you or someone in your bloodline.

s. Legal rights.

t. Curses on you or your bloodline.

u. Add your own sin – Honestly.

4. **Introduce yourself.**

   a. Acknowledge the Righteous Judge as the Father and also as the righteous judge.

   b. What you are and what you do – I am an evangelist.

   c. Who you are – I am privileged to pray for others daily, I am an ambassador for Christ.

   d. I pray daily for this country and others; friends, families, and church members.

   e. I am born again – I received Jesus as my Lord and Savior and He remains my savior.

   f. I am a child of God.

   g. Your word says – If I confess my sins, you are faithful and just to forgive me – 1 John 1:9-10.

   h. I am here today, this evening or morning to confess my sins and the sins of my bloodline and I repent of them all.

5. **Here are what I need you to acquit me of O' Righteous Judge.**

   a. I am not arguing about all the accusations against me.

   b. I am here to ask for mercy and for you to blot my sins away and forgive me.

   c. Here are my sins in addition to all of the accusations in the book before you.

   d. Discharge and acquit me of all charges.

   e. Restore my marriage.

   f. Not Married – I want to get married, because your word says it is not good for a man to be alone.

   g. Restore my finances – Your word says if I cannot provide for my household, I am worse than an infidel and I denied the faith – 1Timothy 5:8.

   h. Restore my generational blessings.

   i. Restore my dream life.

   j. Open my spiritual eyes and ears.

   k. Let my senses become active toward you.

   l. Release my Devine helpers and direct them to find me.

   m. Protect me – So that I continue to do what I do to the glory of your name.

   n. Protect my wife.

   o. Break every covenant entered by me or someone else affecting me.

   p. Protect my children.

   q. Heal me of disease.

   r. Terminate all covenants that are not with you.

   s. Save me from imminent shame.

   t. Remove anger from me or my family members.

   u. Destroy altars that have been raised against me and family members.

   v. Add more of whatever you remember.

6. **Let the book in Hell and Heaven be opened.**
    a. Whatever is in the book in Hell against me be nullified.
    b. Whatever is in the Book in Heaven for me should be established.
    c. Help me begin to live my life according to my book in Heaven.
    d. Stolen dreams by my bloodline – forgive me. (Anyone in my bloodline that stole other people's dreams).
    e. Restore stolen dreams and glory by my bloodline to the owners.
    f. Whatever is in the book in hell against my family members be nullified.

7. **Where to serve copies of this discharge and acquitter judgment?**
    a. Let the judgment I received from you be served in hell.
    b. Let this judgment be served in covens.
    c. Let this judgment be served on evil powers sitting on legal grounds to afflict me.
    d. Let this judgment be served at my residence.
    e. Let this judgment be served at my workplace.
    f. Let this judgment be served on anyone who has legal rights to do me harm.
    g. Let this judgment be served on anyone who has legal rights to cause harm on my wife or children.
    h. Father Lord, let this judgment be served on the universe to be seen by any powers that are holding legal standing to do evil against me.